Distributed Object Technology: Concepts and Applications

Hewlett-Packard Professional Books

Distributed Object Technology: Concepts and Applications

Timothy W. Ryan

Hewlett-Packard Company

To join a Prentice Hall PTR internet mailing list,
point to: **http://www.prenhall.com/register**

Prentice Hall PTR, Upper Saddle River, NJ 07458
http://www.prenhall.com

Library of Congress Cataloging-in-Publication Data

Ryan, Tim, 1957-
Distributed object technology: concepts and applications / by Tim
Ryan
    p. cm. (Hewlett-Packard professional books)
    Includes bibliographical references and index.
    ISBN 0-13-348996-5
    1. Object-oriented methods (Computer science).   2. Distributed
databases. I. Title. II. Series.
QA76.9.O35R93   1996
005.2—dc20   96-32744
                                         CIP

Editorial/Production Supervision: *Eileen Clark*
Cover Design director: *Jerry Votta*
Cover Design: *Talar Agasyon*
Manufacturing Manager: *Alexis Heydt*
Acquisitions Editor: *Karen Gettman*
Editorial Assistant: *Barbara Alfieri*
Manager, Hewlett-Packard Press: *Patricia Pekary*

© 1997 by Hewlett-Packard Company

Published by Prentice Hall PTR
Prentice-Hall, Inc.
A Simon & Schuster Company
Upper Saddle River, New Jersey 07458

The publisher offers discounts on this book when ordered in bulk quantities.
For more information, contact:
         Corporate Sales Department
         Prentice Hall PTR
         One Lake Street
         Upper Saddle River, NJ 07458
         Phone: 800-382-3419 Fax: 201-236-7141
         E-mail: corpsales@prenhall.com

Printed in the United States of America
10 9 8 7 6 5 4 3 2 1

ISBN 0-13-348996-5

Prentice-Hall International (UK) Limited, *London*
Prentice-Hall of Australia Pty. Limited, *Sydney*
Prentice-Hall Canada Inc., *Toronto*
Prentice-Hall Hispanoamericana, S.A., *Mexico*
Prentice-Hall of India Private Limited, *New Delhi*
Prentice-Hall of Japan, Inc., *Tokyo*
Simon & Schuster Asia Pte. Ltd., *Singapore*
Editora Prentice-Hall do Brasil, Ltda., *Rio de Janeiro*

To my beloved Julie, the most wonderful woman I have ever known.

(Prov. 31:25-31)

CONTENTS

FIGURES

ACKNOWLEDGMENTS

Many people have provided significant contributions to the development of this book. Jeff Eastman, the creator and architect of Distributed Smalltalk, gave me much insight and encouragement early on. Joe Sventek has been a great help in pointing me in the right direction. Mary Loomis has been a continual inspiration and guide. Keith Moore, David L. Neumann of NeXT, Colin Newman of IONA Technologies, and others helped shape my understanding of CORBA and of CORBA OLE integration. Doug Dedo, Tu-ting Cheng, and many others helped me gain an appreciation for object persistence.

Thanks to Dave Lange, Bob Stevenson, Mike Short, and many others who provided thoughtful comments on the book. Thanks also to Lynn Wilson, Dave Lange, Stu Perron, Lisa Johnson, Dan Kistner, Jerry Kauffman, and John Bittermann for their roles in the NewWave-based CRW project of several years ago that sparked my initial interest in distributed objects.

Thanks also to Jackie Parker, Steve Wieber, Bob Asmar, Scott Dunt, Steve Beasley, Steve Crowe, and many others at HP for their help and support.

Pat Pekary of HP Press, Karen Gettman, and Eileen Clark of Prentice Hall PTR were extremely helpful and patient in bringing the book to print.

I especially want to thank Julie, Heather, Elisabeth, and Amy for their love, patience, and encouragement while I was off working on this book.

PREFACE

CORBA, OLE, WWW. These acronyms indicate the three centers of gravity for the distributed object universe — the Common Object Request Broker Architecture, Object Linking and Embedding, and the World Wide Web. This universe is one where an individual or a corporation has unprecedented ability to acquire, understand, manipulate, and exploit high-value information and processes. In the distributed object universe, there is the prospect of access to the information we want, when we want it, in the form we want it. Data that until now has been hidden away because of its origin or its location will become more readily available. Processes that are difficult to leverage from one business area to another become much easier to leverage across business boundaries. The ease with which nontechnical users will be able to combine and disseminate information will increase significantly.

Technology companies like Hewlett-Packard, Microsoft, Netscape Communications, and Oracle, as well as information technology consumers such as Citibank and Motorola point to distributed object technology (such as CORBA, OLE, and some of the newer Web technologies) as one of the best paths to making information systems the resource we really need them to be. No one is saying it will be easy, but with the synergy of object technology and distributed client/server computing, we will improve our ability to control and understand information within and between organizations.

In terms of actual implementation technology, nothing compares to the contribution that is being and will be made by Distributed Object Technology (DOT). DOT will change the way we think about computing and networks. It will impact virtually every industry, every application developer, and every user. Along with improvements in lower-level network hardware and software, it will help facilitate the coming multimedia revolution. It will provide significant contributions to managing the information explosion we are currently experiencing. These changes may occur gradually, but they will most certainly occur.

This book is addressed to information systems professionals at many levels. The earlier and later chapters are useful to managers who need to understand the impacts of distributed object computing. The middle chapters are particularly suited to developers who are interested in understanding the basics of DOT.

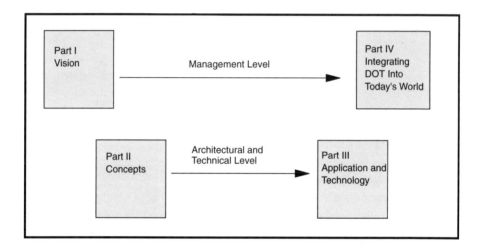

With a nod to Dr. David Taylor and the structure of his book *Object-oriented Information Systems*, this book is structured in distinct layers. Part I sets the stage for the following parts. It discusses the *why* and basic *what* of DOT. Part II goes into more depth on the *what* of DOT. Part III explains in greater detail the most common and robust expressions of DOT. Part IV comes back up to the management level to talk about how DOT is and can be integrated with the rest of today's information systems environment.

The book provides an overview of the concepts at the foundation of distributed object technology. It then illustrates the application of these concepts via examples based on current DOT technology. Part I outlines a vision for the use of DOT. Chapter 1 discusses why users want and need services provided by DOT. It explains the increasing demand for text, graphics, images, and multimedia services that are shared by widely dispersed workgroups collaborating on both simple and complex projects and tasks. This *virtual proximity* is becoming more important as users depend more and more on their information systems as critical components in all of their activities. Chapter 1 also introduces a primary theme of the book: a *vision* for how users would like to see information systems accessed. This scenario for the future will be a unifying factor in how distributed object technology will be presented in the book. Chapter 2 introduces the technology necessary to provide DOT services. Objects organize data and help infuse it with *meaning*. When interfaces, databases, and networks are enhanced with object technology, they are more powerful individually as well as synergistically.

Chapter 3 begins the part that introduces DOT concepts. It discusses how object modeling improves the way computer professionals think when applying information technology to real-world business needs. Chapter 4 covers how graphical user interfaces have significantly improved the usability of computer systems but have not fully exploited the capabilities of object technology. Object-oriented graphical user interfaces (OO GUIs) take the next step in improving user interface usability. Chapter 5 provides a discussion of how object-oriented databases provide context to information. This is in contrast with hierarchical or relational database systems that do a good job of storing or retrieving data but provide very little help with understanding how the data they store can be used. In Chapter 6, the application of object-orientation to networking is explained. Today's networks provide interconnectivity, but require object-oriented developers to give up the tools that work so well for OO GUIs, languages, and databases. OO networks allow developers to extend the usefulness of OO technology across the network without requiring significant additional effort. Chapter 7 brings it all together, integrating interfaces, data bases, and networks in a unified, object-oriented whole. Chapter 8 introduces the concept of Enterprise *Views*. This chapter will focus on how DOT is well-suited to helping users more effectively organize all of the business data that is available to them.

Chapter 9 begins the application part. Chapters 9 through 11 discuss, in a more detailed fashion, how distributed object technology works and has been expressed in various tools. A theme running through these chapters is the vision described in Chapter 1. That vision is of an information systems environment that is difficult, if not impossible, to support using more traditional methods of application development. It is still a challenge, but much more achievable using the kinds of technology described in this book. Many of the technologies available in the distributed object arena are somewhat difficult to grasp at first. To simplify the discussion, relatively simple examples and languages are used for teaching purposes. For CORBA technologies, Smalltalk is an excellent teaching vehicle for many of these concepts. For OLE, Visual Basic provides easy to use and understand interfaces. For the Web, Hypertext Markup Language (HTML) is used.

Chapter 9 discusses CORBA and CORBAservices. It discusses how new information is created in a distributed object environment via Lifecycle services, shows how users will find information in the DOT environment using Naming services, and talks about how DOT supports linking objects, including the value of the containment (or *folder*) model of organizing information. It elaborates on how Event services help distributed objects work together over more extended periods of time and explains how objects can be used in a transaction with Transaction services. It then discusses the Object Request Broker (ORB). The ORB is the *engine* of a CORBA environment. The chapter ends with discussion about how clients and servers need a *contract* in order to work together effectively. The Interface Definition Language (IDL) is the language of this type of contract. This chapter will illustrate how IDL works and its role in the DOT world.

Chapter 10 discusses OLE Remote Automation and how it supports networked objects. Chapter 11 discusses how Universal Resource Locators (URLs), Hypertext Transfer Protocol (HTTP), and HTML are rudimentary distributed object technologies and will be supplemented to more fully utilize the power and flexibility of DOT as found in CORBA and OLE.

Chapter 12 begins the final part, which focuses on how DOT will fit in with current information system technology. The chapter explains how DOT can wrap around mainframe legacy systems to improve maintainability and usability. Chapter 13 shows how Computer-Assisted Software Engineering (CASE) can leverage DOT and how DOT can leverage enterprise modeling. Systems and network management of the DOT infrastructure are presented in Chapter 14.

Perhaps the most significant area of impact for DOT is the corporate culture. Chapter 15 provides guidelines on how organizations may evolve to take advantage of DOT. The final chapter gives some vision of how DOT will affect the wider world of information distribution and usage. For example, how will news and entertainment be influenced by DOT? Chapter 16 offers some perspectives on this question.

Part I

Vision

A vision is a (generally) optimistic view of the future. Often, a vision becomes self-fulfilling, hence its value. Part I presents a vision for how distributed object technology can make a positive contribution to our work environments. It can be hoped that a vision such as the one presented here will become reality for most of us in the not-to-distant future.

1

WHY THE NEED FOR DISTRIBUTED OBJECTS?

CORPORATE AMERICA IS REINVENTING ITS INFORMATION SYSTEMS

A recurring theme heard today is that the only thing that won't change is the fact that everything will continue to change. Even healthy corporations are downsizing, upper management is trying to find ways to *empower* front-line employees, and technology on all fronts is advancing, sometimes radically changing the competitive landscape. In the midst of the battle for survival, companies also find their information systems departments on the critical path or in the way of growth and opportunity. Many CEOs and upper managers ask themselves, "What can be done to our information systems to make them powerful tools in enabling us to meet our customers' needs and advance against the competition, all in the face of continual change?"

One key to surviving is to do more with less. In an era of intense, global competition, those corporations that can produce a better product or more effectively meet a customer's need using fewer resources than their competitors will thrive, while those who can't will find it rough going indeed. As one looks at continuing layoffs at even high-technology companies such as AT&T and Digital Equipment Corporation, it is obvious that what was lean a few years ago may not be lean enough tomorrow.

A corporation's information systems provide it with its institutional memory and its *nervous system*. If, as the corporation grows and adapts, its information systems cannot adapt with it, the growth of the entire organization is impeded. Indeed, some organizations stand to lose market share if they don't keep up with the trends in information systems. "The banking industry stands at the crossroads," according to David Taylor, Executive Vice-President of the Bank Administration Institute and co-director of the study "The Information Superhighway and Retail Banking":

> The online services, software giants, global entertainment companies, telcos, and utilities have the pipelines and the navigation tools. If banks don't act with foresight and firm purpose, the prognosis is for a continuing erosion of their core retail business.

A significant trend in information systems architectures involves breaking down the *silos* between functional areas. In a CSC Consulting Group survey, senior Information Systems (IS) executives ranked "instituting cross-functional information systems" second after "aligning IS and corporate goals."

While many key technologies have emerged that promote development and implementation of more effective and adaptable information systems, one technology that stands with the leaders is Object-Oriented Technology (OOT). OOT provides several benefits to developers and implementers of information systems, one of the most significant being that of facilitating improved reusability. According to Mary Loomis, Director of Software Technology at Hewlett-Packard (HP) Laboratories, object technology helps in building smaller components that can also leverage other components' capabilities. By providing improved reusability, OOT allows a corporation's IS department to spend more time developing new information systems and less time maintaining old ones. OOT also makes information systems more adaptable. With OOT, a new system can be constructed out of object-oriented components that already exist but are rearranged into a new configuration. This is much cheaper than developing a system with entirely new components.

Another significant facet of OOT is encapsulation. Encapsulation means that an object-oriented software component presents a well-defined interface to whomever or whatever wants to use it. The actual method of performing its work (its *implementation*) is hidden. This permits the implementation to be improved or enhanced at a later time without requiring a change in the component's interface or a change within any of the human procedures or computer software used to access it.

A separate dimension in the evolution of information systems that is equally important is the development of client/server technology. The development of intelligent desktop client workstations and high-speed networks have brought unprecedented power and access to the fingertips of information systems users. For example, as appeared on *Business Wire* on Dec. 6, 1995:

> NeXT Computer Inc. today unveiled the Dodge Virtual Showroom, an on-line demonstration that enables consumers to dynamically view and

select options from the entire line of Dodge automobiles and trucks....
A self-guided tour through Dodge's inventory of cars and trucks allows
users to select from the following options: model, color, price, option
packages, and financing — creating a custom page on-the-fly to reflect
users' selections.

Intelligent desktop client workstations allow even nontechnical end users the
capability to manipulate data in ways undreamed of a decade ago. There are software
tools for data manipulation, data visualization, computation, information presentation, and data integration that enable users of intelligent clients to more quickly and
effectively use and communicate important company and organizational information.

The kinds of applications that need to be available to access physically and geographically distributed information have not kept up with the needs of users, however.
It is not trivial for end users to effectively share information that is processed so con-
veniently on a single intelligent client. There are indications that object technology,
combined with networking infrastructures such as the World Wide Web, are synergistic. For example, "Objects and the Web are inextricably linked," said Bill Lyons, Pres-
ident and CEO of ParcPlace-Digitalk (*Newsbytes News Network*, December 1, 1995).
We'll explore just how objects and networking technology work together to help meet
the significant challenges faced by corporate IS staffs today.

WHAT USERS OF INFORMATION SYSTEMS DREAM ABOUT

Several years ago, I was involved in a prototyping project with a large financial services client. This prototype used HP NewWave and other tools to prototype a futur-
istic financial services application. The prototype illustrated the power of distributed
objects — an integrated OO desktop connected to information that was widely distributed, yet accessed rather easily. Once we developed this prototype, which was
kind of a *concept car* of how the future would look, I became interested in learning
more about the kind of technology that would need to be available behind the scenes
to make the kind of desktop we had imagined become reality. The content of this
book is the essence of what I discovered.

In general, a prototype is a significant aid in understanding the business value
of technology. By developing business scenarios and playing those scenarios through
a prototype which evolves iteratively, a more complete understanding of how technologies can work together to meet a business need is gained. This book, in fact, uses
that idea to illustrate distributed object technology and its business value. In this chapter a business scenario integrated with information technology is presented. The technology used in the scenario exists today in various forms, although as of this writing,
it is not as well integrated as in the scenario. The use of different technologies is partly

to bring out some of the power and strengths of each, as well as to more fully illustrate what is possible today.

THE SCENARIO

Amy is a development manager for a medium-sized manufacturing firm called WorldView Industries. This firm develops custom hardware and software, as well as provides links to video *content providers* to help cable television and phone companies provide video-on-demand services for its customers (see the sidebar on George Gilder's insightful comments on the *telecomputer*). While she has *line* duties to make sure various projects are kept on schedule, she is occasionally called upon to support the sales force in their efforts to customize the firm's products for specialized markets.

Amy has a high-resolution, 21-inch monitor attached to her intelligent client. Her monitor also has a touch-sensitive membrane over it. Right in front of Amy is an ergonomic keyboard with a trackball. Her workstation is attached to WorldView's internal network via a 100 megabit lan card. WorldView's internal network is attached to the global Internet via several gateway machines.

GEORGE GILDER'S TELECOMPUTER — THE REPLACEMENT FOR THE TELEVISION

"TV broadcasters have been the world's biggest air hogs. With no alternative technology in sight and few competing uses for the air, however, television has not until now had to justify its immense demands for spectrum. But in the 1980s, just as the microchip had transformed the dimensions of electronics, fiber optics reshaped the possibilities of all media. The limitations of the air and even of the coaxial copper wires that carry cable television, gave way to the unlimited bandwidth of lasers and glass. Fiber-optic glass wires, the width of a human hair, could potentially bear billions or even trillions of characters of information per second... .

"Like all technologies superseded by more powerful inventions, television (will) not readily disappear... . But the fate of technologies is defined not by their prevalence, but by their competitiveness and promise... .

"The new system will be the telecomputer, a personal computer adapted for video processing and connected by fiber-optic threads to other telecomputers all around the world. Using a two-way system of signals like telephones do, rather than broadcasting one-way like TV, the telecomputer will surpass the television in video communication just as the telephone surpassed the telegraph in verbal communication."

"Life After Television" – George Gilder, pp. 29-31

To start her work session, Amy presses her finger on an icon showing an In Tray (Figure 1–1). This action opens a window that takes up about half of the lower-left quadrant of the screen. In the In-tray are several new items. There are project status reports from the previous day and week. There are schedule reports indicating when various vendors will be shipping supplies for the production lines for products her group has developed. There are several management reports and requests for information from her peers and superiors. Each of these *reports* are links to data sources in the company's databases.

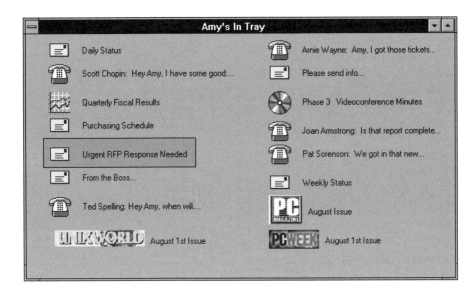

Figure 1–1. In Tray showing electronic mail, voice mail, and links to on-line magazines.

Also in the In Tray are several periodicals that Amy receives. These are represented as miniature images of their logos. These *magazines* are actually just links to the actual *pages* of the magazine that are stored back on the magazine publishers' servers. The pages of the magazines themselves also have links to their base reference sources and to related information. There are a few reports from other areas in her company. There is a memo from her boss. She hears a soft, alarmlike tone that draws her attention to a document from a remote co-worker that has a red box flashing around it, indicating its urgent nature. There are several voice mail calls, each represented by a telephone icon and text indicating the sender and the first two sentences of the contents. Finally, there is an icon representing a ten-minute video clip that contains the highlights of an important meeting held yesterday which Amy had to miss due to a more important conflict. The meeting was actually a video conference of people in several parts of the world. The video clip is presented from the perspective of the coordinator of the conference. The clip is linked to the minutes of the meeting in *hypertext* fashion. That is, by clicking on an area of the minutes, the video clip is positioned at that point in the conference. The clip also has links to documentation that was related to the meeting.

Amy has a calendar object on her screen. Amy clicks on her calendar object, showing a week-per-page view (Figure 1–2). Each day has several meetings on it. Some of the meetings have been placed there by other people and have shaded boxes around them. The shaded box indicates that the text about the meeting is actually a *view*. This view contains a link back to the originator's calendar. If the originator of the meeting changes the meeting information, the information automatically changes on Amy's calendar as well. If Amy clicks on a given meeting box, a window would open with all of the information currently known about that meeting.

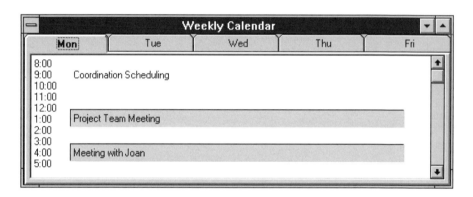

Figure 1–2. Calendar showing appointments are *linked* to another person's calendar. When the highlighted appointments are updated, they are updated for everyone linked to that appointment.

In her In Tray, Amy presses on the document with the flashing red box first. A window opens up, taking up 30 percent of her screen, right in the middle. It is a message from Heather in Sales (Figure 1–3). The text of the message indicates that Amy's company has an opportunity to close a significant deal with a large client if they can present the right business strategy and line up the appropriate resources in a short time period. Attached to the text is the client's Request For Proposal (RPF), a profile of the client, a list of the people from Amy's company already involved, the current draft of the business strategy, and a request for the kind of aid needed from Amy's department. Amy looks at the clock, noting that she has a production meeting in 45 minutes. She doesn't have much time to help Heather, but she can give her the next half hour.

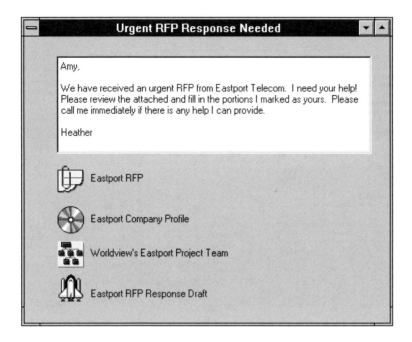

Figure 1–3. Electronic mail message containing introductory text and reference links to objects on distributed servers that reside both on the company's intranet and the Internet.

Amy presses her finger on the icon containing the request for proposal, scans it once, and then reads it more carefully. She then presses the icon containing the profile of the client and is presented with a window containing text, video, and graphics (Figure 1–4). She presses the *Start* button in the window, and the video begins. The video is of a man describing various aspects of the client company. It turns out to be the company's annual report, multimedia style. As the video plays, the text and graphics displays that are next to the video window track along with the video images. The text on the left of the video depicts what the man says, along with footnotes that the man doesn't refer to. The graphics display on the right of the video presents charts, diagrams, and images that support the discussion in the video. There is also a window containing several icons that allow the user to pause, speed up, and start/stop the video. Since Amy doesn't have much time, she fast forwards through several areas of the video. Since it is actually a digital image on disk, she can move back and forth, scanning the video, the text, and the graphics for information that is of use to her.

Amy runs the video all the way through once. She then runs through it again, placing electronic *bookmarks* in the places that she thinks she'll need to refer to again

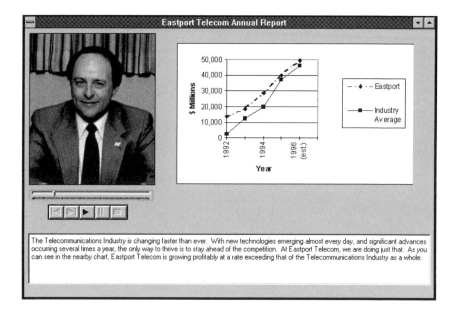

Figure 1–4. Annual report object. As the video plays, the narrative text and charts are updated accordingly.

later. Amy then reviews the list of people involved. She sees her name on the list, as well as four others, all department heads. "Must really be important," she says to herself. She opens up the current draft of the business strategy and an outline that was put together by Heather in Sales. It contains numerous pages filled in by other departments, while the areas that are her department's responsibility are still blank. Each portion of the outline has a notation indicating the person or department responsible for that portion. These notations are cross-linked to the list of involved parties.

Amy is particularly interested in the section developed by Beth in Research. She presses on Beth's name and a window opens in the upper-right-hand corner of her desktop. It is black with the words *Ringing* in white in the center of the window. A moment later the words read *Answered,* and then an image of Beth appears. She is wearing her glasses today. She must have been up late reading last night, since Amy knows she wears her contacts unless her eyes are tired.

Amy and Beth discuss the current status of the project. They leaf through the current draft together. As either one of them turns pages or highlights words or graphics, the document on the desk of the other one reflects the action, just as if they were sitting at a conference table leafing through a single copy together. After Amy and Beth confer for 15 minutes, the draft is several pages thicker and contains many more charts and graphics, pulled mostly from Beth's research databases. The research databases Beth is using were put together by both the company's research department and standard industry reference sources. (In this scenario, the reference sources aren't just books or even on-line databases. They are network-ready object-oriented repositories that allow a user to create persistent links from desktop objects to everything from a simple paragraph or picture to an entire *book* on most subjects.) Several key additions are made from the client company's own annual report, however, which Amy had bookmarked. Amy has found that the best way to show her company's value is by directly relating its services, as often as possible, to the client company's business objectives. Amy links the bookmarked sections of the annual report to her company's proposal via *hot links*. Therefore, if the client wants to see the original source of Amy's inclusions, double-clicking on the entry will bring up that section of the annual report.

Amy and Beth say their farewells and Amy closes the connection to Beth. Amy looks at the clock. She still has 15 minutes until her project meeting. She sits back, sips her still warm coffee, and reflects that it's a good thing that Beth is only six time zones away, so she was still at work when Amy called.

At this point, the scenario ends. Imagine what would need to take place to give Amy the power to access information as she did in her work session. Much of the remainder of this book will be devoted to explaining some of the key software technologies that will enable the kind of capabilities in the scenario above to become reality.

First, look at what actually would have happened to Amy and her co-workers without the kind of technology in the scenario. How much longer would the scenario have taken with the technology that is pervasive today?

1. Much of the information Amy used in her collaboration with Beth and Heather would have been given to her in paper format, probably dropped in her in tray.
2. The creation of the business strategy paper would have required reentering data from the client company's annual report.
3. Any charts or graphs would have to have been reproduced, at some time and cost.
4. Her conversation with Beth would have been made more difficult by the distance between them.
5. Beth's research results would likely have been faxed to Amy, and she and Beth would have needed to confer over the phone.
6. It is possible that they would have misunderstood some of the kinds of additions each was making to the report, causing confusion and possible delays.
7. It is also possible that the kind of collaboration required may have required air travel by one of them, significantly extending the time of the project and impact on their individual schedules.

Two key aspects of Amy's session were, first, that information was presented in its most natural format, whether text, audio, video, or graphics, and second, that it was very easy to take pieces of information from one source and link them to another source. What we will explore is how advances in software technology via distributed object technology and related technologies will also enable Amy to achieve this kind of access and control of information.

Let's analyze Amy's session from an information systems perspective.

RAPID HETEROGENEOUS DATA ACCESS

During the collaboration, information access was transparent. The location of the data was invisible to the users. This location invisibility or *encapsulation* is a key aspect of distributed object technology The data being accessed may have been either from a single source or from local copies of the information. Data replication can be viewed as a form of caching — keeping remotely updated information stored in a local copy. However, there is great benefit in accessing a particular type of data from a single data source, regardless of where the accessor is. While replication has its merits, especially in improving performance of access times, it also introduces the need for keeping replicated copies synchronized. Simple caching of information that is pulled in from a remote server at the time that information is accessed also improves performance, without all of the difficulties of replication. Updates are best performed against a single master copy of the original information, with the caches refreshing themselves as needed.

With distributed object systems, the type of hardware, operating system, network, etc., is less a factor in enabling access to data than it is with some other technologies. Assume, for example, that the company annual report that Amy read was actually on the client company's own server, which was one hardware/ operating system platform. With DOT, Amy's own servers and clients can be of another platform, but she would be able to access not only the network of that company but also use the higher level services presented by the annual report, such as coordination of the video, charting, and text streams of data that were connected via such technologies as an object event service.

SYSTEMS THAT SERVE (VERY FRIENDLY INTERFACES)

Amy was presented with screens that were easy to navigate. Graphical User Interfaces (GUIs) are a key enabling technology in making systems easy to access. GUIs can provide metaphors that make the computer appear to match what the end user has in mind when accessing information. A GUI can paint a desktop, an office, a notebook, or even a playground on the screen — presenting objects that the user can access and interact with. Distributed object technology is a key enabler behind the scenes to make a graphical client workstation effective at accessing information that may not be on the user's local client machine. A current limitation of many GUI screens is that the ease of use is only skin deep. Once a user wants to access information that is not located in the file or database system of the local machine, the user has to find it, figure out what kind of data it is, run the proper program to access it, etc.

Further, if there are different types of information that a user wants to access from several different machines, the GUI alone does little to aid in the integration of that information. Distributed object technology facilitates providing information to the user in a *richly semantic* form. That is, it provides high-value information that also *understands* how it can integrate itself with other information. For example, in Amy's session, she was able to access various types of information, text, video, sound, and *views* of text from one document embedded in another document, seamlessly and easily. She didn't need to know that at one moment she was dealing with a word processing application or with a sound file application or with a video application or with an e-mail package. The different applications were integrated, and the data they accessed was linked together in a transparent fashion.

SYSTEMS WITH NO PHYSICAL BOUNDARIES (TRANSPARENT AND SCALABLE DISTRIBUTION)

Collaboration doesn't need to be real time or over large distances to benefit from this type of technology. Even if Amy and Beth were in the same office complex and the collaboration took place over a period of hours or days, the efficiency and quality of the work they were sharing would be improved by distributed object technology. The benefit from DOT was that Beth and Amy were able to see exactly the same thing, right down to their own *pencil* marks on the screens, in real time, and in the same way. There was little room for error in the presentation of the materials due to incorrect or unmatched versions of documents, misunderstandings of what was being looked at, etc.

APPLICATION LINKING AND EMBEDDING

The annual report that Amy accessed was actually a compound object that consisted of several *component objects* that were linked together. The *component objects* kept in step with each other while they *played* via an object event service, which will be discussed later. The way it worked was like this: The annual report actually consisted of three basic objects; a video object, a text object, and a chart object. The video object was wrapped around the video stream which showed the man discussing the company's products and performance. As the video played, a counter was updated with the number of *frames* that had been played. The object wrapped around the video stream kept track of the number of *frames* that had passed by. When a certain frame count had been reached, the video wrapper object sent *event* messages to the two other objects. In this case, the video wrapper object was an *event supplier*, while the text and graphics objects were *event consumers*.

The text and graphics objects would simply wait until they received event messages from the video wrapper object before they would change their screens from one page or one chart to the next. As the video progressed, the video wrapper would send events to the other two objects, which would *flip their pages* in concert with the video wrapper as they received the event messages. This synchronization could have coordinated many more than just three objects. Event services can permit the use of an *event channel* that funnels events from multiple event suppliers to multiple event consumers.

Note that these events need not just be *turn the page messages*. The events are objects in themselves and may contain a substantial amount of information. The events could have contained higher-level semantics, such as subject-page combinations, or even an outline of the overall report (Figure 1–5). The events, in effect, could

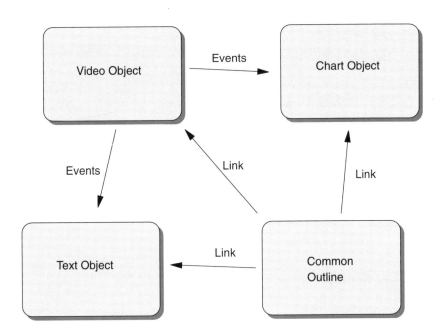

Figure 1–5. Component structure of the annual report object. It consists of three objects connected by events and sharing a common outline.

have said, "display a particular graph or table," or "go to this heading" on a common outline. In this way, the video could have been stopped or moved backward and forward manually, with the two supporting objects, the text and the charts, moving backward and forward in conjunction with the video.

This is an extremely powerful abstraction. At the user's command, linked information is navigated back and forth in real time. This has value for historical information like operational data, such as customer information, where the customer is linked to orders and shipments, etc. Remember, since the event linking the objects is an object itself, there are many models of link *semantics* that can be brought together to define the links' behavior. Starting from simple *record IDs*, moving up to much more businesslike linkage semantics, many possibilities exist for use of this type of service.

TASK-ORIENTED DESKTOPS

Note that in the session, Amy never worried about what *application* she was running. She simply pointed at the object she wanted to access, and the application that it used was loaded automatically. This allowed Amy to focus on her job, not on the particular program or application she was using. For example, Amy didn't have to think in order to run a program to access her electronic mail, she just saw an in tray icon and clicked on it. Also, when she wanted to look at Heather's message, she simply clicked on it and it opened. When the annual report was accessed, she just double-clicked on it. While most operating systems allow a simple file, like a spreadsheet or word processing document, to be associated with a program, there is generally no provision for *programs within a program*, for example, a spreadsheet within a word processing document within an e-mail program — especially if the data for each of these programs is on different server machines. OLE is a technology that supports this kind of distributed compound document need.

Distributed object technology frees a user more than ever before from being constrained by their understanding of applications and their server network. It allows the users to focus more on the task at hand rather than on the technology.

2

WHAT IS DISTRIBUTED OBJECT TECHNOLOGY?

Distributed object technology is the synergistic application of object-oriented principles to distributed, network-oriented application development and implementation. As visionaries like Patricia Seybold have recognized for many years, objects and networks were made for each other. DOT brings location transparency and seamless integration of different technologies.

In the simplest terms, DOT is the encapsulation of data and functions into objects with the further encapsulation of location. That is, to access information, a user or application doesn't need to know whether it is accessing simple stored data or a possibly complex function. In addition, the user or application doesn't need to know whether the information is on the local computer or a remote one.

There are three primary aspects of how object technology applies to distributed applications. These areas are Graphical User Interface (GUI)-based clients, networks, and application servers. Before we address each of these specific areas, let us review some of the more important aspects of object technology itself.

THE POWER OF OBJECTS

Everyone is familiar with the term *Animal Kingdom.* It represents the organization of animals into a hierarchy of categories. The top category is mammals, and at the top of that category is people. Next follow birds, reptiles, etc., down to the lowliest invertebrate. The formal name for the study of the structure of the animal kingdom is *taxonomy*, which means, effectively, *classification*, or ordering into categories and sub-categories of greater and lesser importance. All of the creatures in the animal kingdom share some things in common, such as mobility, reproduction, etc. More specific classes of animals, like mammals, share more in common, such as live birth, hair, or fur, etc. In object terms, it may be stated, for example, that humans possess traits that exist in all of the other classes of animals plus some of our own. In the abstract, we *inherit* everything from basic *animal* traits such as simple mobility, reproduction, and nuclei in our cells, through possession of the circulatory and digestive systems, etc., on up to vertebrae, and finally, to the one thing we alone possess, human intelligence. So, also, in the animal kingdom are *types* or *classes* of things available to animals, some of which all animals possess, and some of which only humans possess.

Business information has the same kind of structure. At the base of the *kingdom* in any business are the few key types (or *classes)* of information that are critical to understanding the whole business. For an automobile manufacturer, these would be things like *vehicle* or *people*. *Vehicle* then becomes *car, truck,* then *Taurus, Sable* etc. *People* becomes *customer, dealer, employee,* then *fleet customer, new customer, automotive designer, automobile repairman,* etc.

This organization of *business objects* is quite natural and is at the heart of object-oriented thinking and technology. For object-oriented systems to be successful, they must take advantage of this natural ordering, from the general to the specific.

Another key aspect of object-oriented systems is the notion of cooperation between objects. Since objects are *active data*, they can begin to *cooperate* with one another without having been specifically designed to do so. A spreadsheet object, for example, may have been designed to communicate with a bar chart object. A pie chart object comes along, however, which the spreadsheet object was not originally designed to be able to access. If the pie chart object supports the appropriate interfaces for interaction, however, the spreadsheet object will still be able to interact and *cooperate* with the pie chart object (Figure 2–1).

The final aspect of object technology to discuss is how object orientation provides freedom from *shared data state* via the method of *interface encapsulation.* Shared data state is the situation where a database table, for example, is accessed by several different application programs. These programs all understand the format of the table, and any changes to the table format need to be accounted for in each of the application programs. This may be a particularly sticky problem if the application programs are maintained by diverse, geographically dispersed workgroups.

Object technology solves this problem by encapsulating the data records with object interfaces. Since a particular data item or collection of data items can only be accessed via the published interface, the internal organization of the data becomes invisible to the application programs that access it. As long as the interface to the

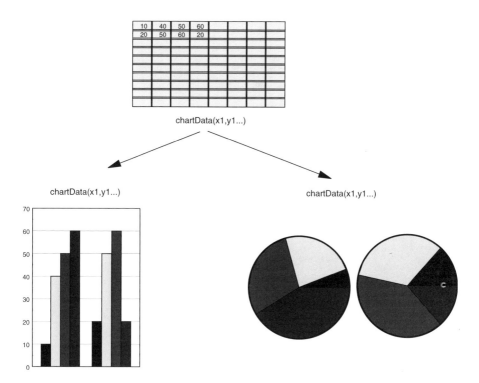

Figure 2–1. Tabular information represented in two different chart styles. Each chart has the same interface but performs different functions on the data.

data remains constant, the format underneath may be changed as needs dictate. While relational databases provide *views*, to help in the hiding of changes in table format to the readers of data, programs that update the data still need to access the base table formats. It may be said, at any rate, that the *views* relational databases provide are a use of encapsulation, an object concept.

Encapsulation is also important in application programs. A simple example comparing a problem solved in COBOL versus Smalltalk will draw this out. For this example, assume a charting application. This application is originally developed to take a set of x, y values and draw either a pie chart or a bar chart. The COBOL program is outlined in Figure 2–2. While the program works, it must explicitly distinguish between the types of charts in the application logic. This is fine until a new type of chart is requested, a line chart. Now, not only must the new procedure to draw a line chart be developed, it is also necessary to modify the control module to recognize a line chart request and call the appropriate procedure (Figure 2–3).

```
*  Draw a chart with the parameters entered

*  Read input

Call "Getvals" giving x-y-array, chart-type.

*  Draw chart

If chart-type = 'bar' then
      call 'Drawbar' using x-y-array
Else if chart-type = 'pie' then
      call 'Drawpie' using x-y-array.

end-program.
```

Figure 2–2. COBOL code fragment to distinguish between two chart functions.

```
*  Draw a chart with the parameters entered

*  Read input

      Call "Getvals" giving x-y-array, chart-type.

*  Draw chart

      If chart-type = 'bar' then
            call 'Drawbar' using x-y-array
      Else if chart-type = 'pie' then
            call 'Drawpie' using x-y-array
      Else if chart-type = 'line' then
            call 'Drawline' using x-y-array.
```

Figure 2–3. COBOL code fragment now includes additional chart function.

This problem is avoided in the Smalltalk program. In this example, three types/classes of objects are created (Figure 2–4). Each is a drawing object, which is subclassed into bar chart and pie chart classes. A given chart is associated with one or the other type of chart. When the chart needs to be drawn, the same method is invoked on either of the objects, which then draws itself. The control program doesn't need to select which function to call. It is handled by the *magic* of pointers, as shown in Figure 2–5. When a new type of chart is needed, it is simply created as another subclass. If the object needed to be drawn is of the new subtype, the same message can be sent to it and it will draw itself. (Figure 2–6 shows the LineChart class being added to the application.) Other parts of the program that need to draw this type of chart don't need to be significantly changed, since the object knows what kind of class it belongs to and invokes the appropriate methods when it receives a message.

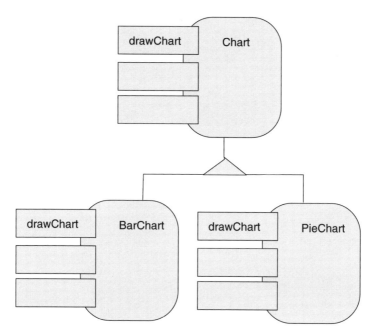

Figure 2–4. Diagram showing inheritance between a *Chart* superclass and *BarChart* and *PieChart* subclasses.

An additional benefit of this approach is that the new class also inherits functionality from the superclass. For example, superclass methods may provide support for assigning colors to parts of the chart, or provide methods for creation of polygons, etc. These methods may be used directly by the new class or subclassed to provide more refined functionality. This type of thing is more difficult to do in third-generation languages like COBOL.

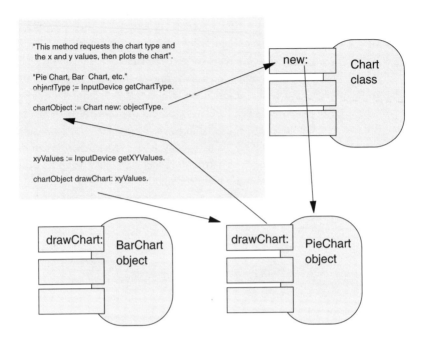

Figure 2–5. Interaction between Chart superclass and PieChart subclass for the *new:* method. Also shown is the *drawChart:* method being executed by the PieChart class.

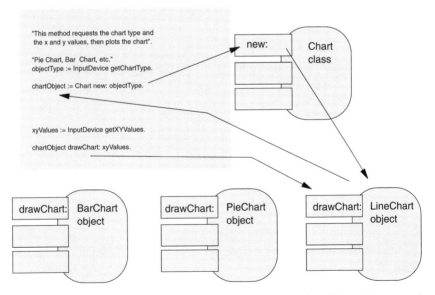

Figure 2–6. LineChart class added to example. If LineChart is selected, it can be accessed without needing to change the code in the example.

At a technical level, all that an object-oriented language is doing is bringing more sophisticated pointer manipulation to the control flow in an application, just as databases brought sophisticated (but easy-to-use) pointer manipulation to data organization in data storage.

OOCLIENTS, OOSERVERS, AND OONETWORKS

The user interface is the place where it is the most obvious that things have come a long way from the days of 80-by-24 green-character display tubes. User interfaces have gained much benefit from object technology. Windowing systems on workstations and PCs would be hard pressed to perform their functions if each window and sub-window (control, button, icon) were not object based. (Object-based means that a technology has some of the attributes of object technology, such as encapsulation of function and data. Object-based technology may lack more sophisticated features of object-oriented systems such as inheritance and polymorphism.) These software components typically utilize encapsulation, have an event-driven control paradigm, and often use some form of inheritance or containment. These features give them an object flavor.

The evolution of the intelligent client and graphical user interface has led to the ability of developers to allow for much more significant customization to the desktop environments they create for end users. It is now routine for end users to organize their graphical *desktops* in a manner natural to their jobs and personalities. This ability to *customize the interface* makes the computer interface appear friendlier and easier to use. This improved ease of use, coming at the hands of windows and icons with customization capabilities, may be attributed to the application of object technology to desktop clients.

Object technology has had an impact on networks as well. Initially, LAN servers stored only simple files (Figure 2–7). Indeed, today, a large number of LAN-based servers still only store simple files. Any real processing to be done on the data in these files is performed on the client. The next step in the evolution is the ability to access relational databases on LAN-based servers. This moves more of the low-level data access function to the server but leaves the real application processing on the client. The third step is the stored procedure or Remote Procedure Call (RPC). This functionality allows more, or even most, of the work to be performed on the server. This *three-tiered* capability is important, in that more complex work may be done on the server and therefore shared equally by all of the clients accessing that server. Since some functionality is associated with the data on a server, some RPC-based servers may be viewed as object-based.

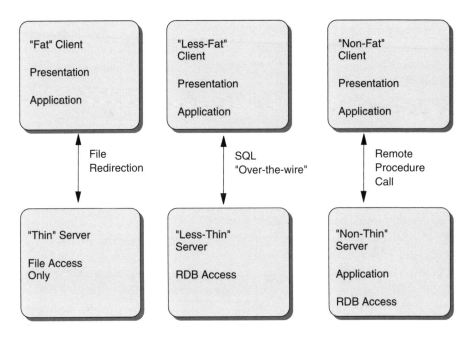

Figure 2–7. Three modes of client/server network interaction. The application can be primarily on the client, the server, or present on both.

The highest step in this evolution thus far is the object-oriented server (Figure 2–8). This is a server that by some means exposes an object-oriented interface to its clients. The server may be implemented using an object-oriented database, or perhaps a relational data base with an object-oriented application program between the database and the network. This server improves on the previous step by allowing a particular client to create a very complex set of objects through relatively few transactions, and then storing that complex object set without *reducing* it to more simple components. For example, a user may build a representation of a *car* entirely from scratch using computer-generated *parts*, perhaps a *Corvette* (Figure 2–9). This car may be stored as a single, complex object on the server. Another user may come along later and access the car object in its entire complexity, merely by accessing the base object *Corvette*. Figure 2–9 represents use of a complex server object that simulates the real world. While somewhat artificial, it graphically illustrates how a server object contains not just complex data relationships, but also complex function interactions.

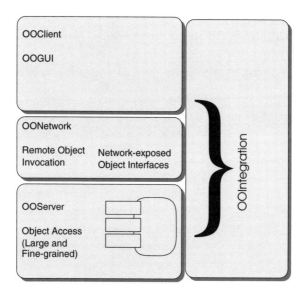

Figure 2–8. Model showing OOClient, OONetwork, and OOServer integration.

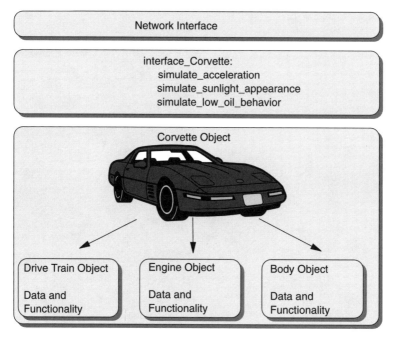

Figure 2–9. Interface to a complex object. The Corvette object consists of numerous other objects that interact and simulate the behavior of the *real-world* object they represent. As the component objects interact, they combine to simulate how the complex object would react.

DISTRIBUTED USER METAPHOR:
BUILDINGS, OFFICES, DESKTOPS, PEOPLE, AND THINGS.

Virtual Proximity: The Basis for Collaborative Work

No man is an island, entire of itself; every man is a piece of the conti-
nent, a part of the main. (John Donne, Meditation 17, from *Devotions
upon Emergent Occasions*).

To be effective, knowledge workers must work closely together. This is a difficult challenge even when they are in close proximity — adjoining offices, different
floors of the same building, the building across the street. The challenge becomes
much greater when knowledge workers must collaborate across town or different time
zones. Numerous means exist, some primitive, some technically sophisticated, to ease
the burden of remote collaboration. Phones, electronic mail, faxes, and even video
teleconferencing only go so far in reducing the challenge of dealing with others who
are physically remote.

Distributed Object Technology makes additional progress in this area. An
object-oriented client can present information in many different formats. One format
that appears to have promise for many knowledge workers is the metaphor of buildings, office, desktops, people, and things (Figure 2–10).

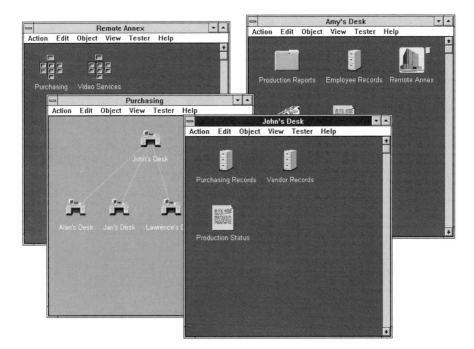

Figure 2–10. Navigation to another person's *Desk*.

This metaphor is familiar to office workers and makes navigation through a distributed system more simple. For one worker, Amy, for example, to access the documents of John, a remote co-worker, she merely

1. chooses the correct building from a set of buildings,
2. chooses the correct office within the building,
3. chooses the right desk in that office, and
4. accesses the appropriate *thing* (file, etc) from the desktop or desk drawer (assuming the appropriate security — that she has a *key* to the appropriate *drawer*).

Since this metaphor matches what Amy would have to do in the real world to access John's documents, it is a natural one for Amy to follow.

THE UNIVERSAL, YET PERSONAL, FILING CABINET

This metaphor can be carried further. At Julie's desk, she has a small filing cabinet. These are her files. Not far from her desk are several larger filing cabinets. These files belong to Julie's workgroup. More and more, however, Julie is storing *files* not in her desk, but in her file area on her workgroup's file server. There is also a shared file area for the files of Julie's local workgroup. This *shared file* area makes it much easier to find things, since Julie doesn't have to leave her desk.

There are limitations to the *shared file area*, however. A simple file server file system is not the optimal way to store every kind of information. It works fine for small numbers of word processing, spreadsheet, and graphics files. It doesn't work well for very large numbers of such files or for such data as scanned images, database records, or any data that must be retrieved through an application. As the quantity of information grows, the complexity of storing and retrieving the information grows with it. What Julie needs is a universal, yet personal, filing cabinet. The contents of this cabinet would be everything that is of interest to her given her position and responsibilities.

This filing cabinet would contain information that she created. It would also contain information that others in Julie's workgroup, whether they are local or remote, created. It would contain information on company policies that are relevant to her job. It would contain industry-related information, government information, technical information, information from universities, the media, any source of information that would be of use to her in her job. The World Wide Web is a current access vehicle for much of this type of information. The Web is a step in the right direction but has some limitations. These will be discussed later.

Such a filing cabinet would take a great deal of space, not to mention putting it together and maintaining it. At least, if it was a physical filing cabinet. But what if it was a *virtual* filing cabinet? What if, as in Amy's session in the first chapter, it was information accessible entirely through your object-oriented client? The only data that you have locally is your own personal data. All other information is accessed via *links* that are kept locally but point to information that resides on object-oriented servers throughout your company and the world. DOT is bringing this sort of filing cabinet to your desktop.

Virtual In Trays and Conference Rooms

A transformation like that of the filing cabinet above is coming to our in trays. Historically, an in tray is a basket on your desk that people drop paper into. To a large and growing segment of the work force, an in tray is also something on your computer that people drop electronic messages into. These in trays will grow in importance until they substantially replace the basket on you desk. Like Amy's in tray in the first chapter, our in trays of the future will accept information in whatever form is most natural to us. If a document is dropped in our virtual in tray that contains not just text, but newspaper clippings, handwritten scrawls, sticky notes, or even live action video clips, no problem.

Faxing documents to remote co-workers and then discussing them over the phone is an effective means of remote collaboration. The logical extension to this is active sharing of a single document via a *shared forum.* This type of facility allows two or more people to share a document or set of documents in an interactive setting (Figure 2–11).

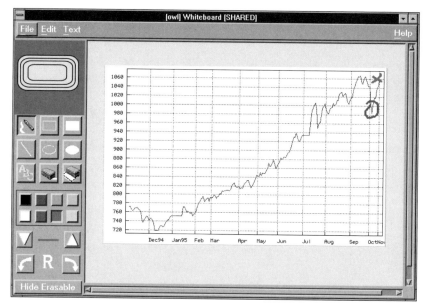

Figure 2–11. Mock-up of a shared *forum* for displaying objects to be viewed in a remote collaboration session.

It works as follows. Peter needs to discuss a document with Laura. He calls Laura on the phone and then opens up the *forum object* on his workstation. He *shares* this object with Laura and it appears on her desktop workstation as well. He then *drags* the relevant document from its place on his workstation screen to the forum. The screen is then visible to both him and Laura. They can each make changes to the document that are visible to the other. They can also add other types of documents to the original in the shared forum and those are visible as well (Figure 2–12). This sort of facility enhances understanding and the finished document is accessible to both of them in a very presentable form.

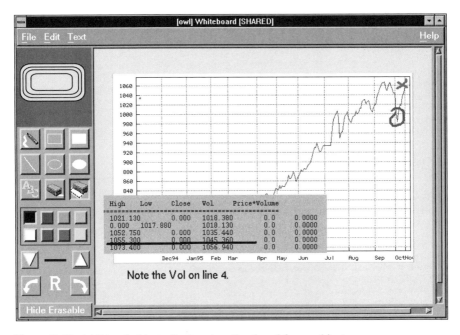

Figure 2–12. Additional objects displayed on the shared forum object.

ELECTRONIC BUSINESS CARDS (USER OBJECTS)

The e-mails of the future will not be complete without an electronic business card. These objects contain not only the name of the person but may also provide direct links to that person's desktop. Using the business card, someone's desktop machine can do everything from dialing the phone to accessing available files from that person. For example, Mark could send an electronic document to Alan over a network and include his business card. This business card contains the usual information about Mark but also contains a *hot link* to the original document in Mark's electronic files. If Alan needs an updated copy of the document, he can access it via Mark's card.

ATLAS MEETS MERCURY (*MAPS* TO *TRAVEL* THE INFORMATION HIGHWAY)

Just as we use an atlas to navigate automobile highways, we will find that maps will be very important to travel the information highway. Since we are traveling the electronic highways at lightning speeds, however, we can move over these data thoroughfares like the mythical Mercury. Such maps may be represented as menus, HTML documents, geographic information systems (sensitive maps), or whatever model suits the type of information. For example, information on the specifications for an airplane may be spread out on servers throughout the world. The initial *menu* for this information may be presented as a model of the airplane (Figure 2–13). To access more detailed information, the user might *click* on a section or component of the airplane. The component (i.e., object) activated would know where its

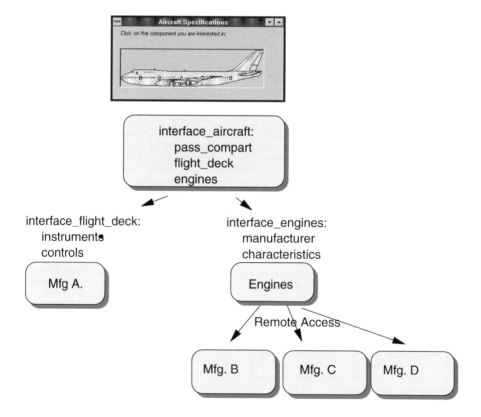

Figure 2–13. Complex object made up of distributed objects. The *interface_aircraft* provides access to component objects, some of which are on other companies' servers.

detailed information was kept. It would then send a message to the remote location where the detailed information for that component is located, asking that the information display itself on the user's screen. Since the component/object itself knows where its detailed information is kept, the user is freed from needing to know that information.

This is a sample of the kind of power inherent in an object-oriented *map* or model used to navigate a distributed information system or highway. The user only needs to know what he wants; the system is then responsible for finding the information, wherever it is.

Part II

Concepts

Part II discusses some of the key concepts behind object technology in general, and distributed object technology in particular. It lays the foundation for the Part III (Applications) and gives some structure to the kinds of considerations that need to be made as users and developers work toward the vision discussed in Part I.

3

OBJECT MODELS

A model is an abstract description of the real world. It is a simplified representation of more complex forms, processes, and functions of physical phenomena or ideas.

– Moshe F. Rubinstein, *Patterns of Problem Solving*, Prentice Hall, 1975.

Object modeling is a strong step toward giving application developers the tools they need to support enterprise applications more effectively. Object analysis allows a user and a developer to communicate about a business problem in business terms. Since no substantial transformations occur in an object model between analysis, through design and implementation a user can more easily comprehend how an application designed with OO analysis and design will match a business need. This chapter will discuss the state of the art in OO modeling and discuss its future in the world of distributed OO modeling. Most of the chapter's figures use the Fusion method notation. Fusion, which was the work of Derek Coleman and his team at HP Laboratories in Bristol, England, was the first *second-generation* OO modeling methodology, especially in that it took from the best of the first-generation methods to create a *fused*, unified method. Derek set off a trend because, since then, consolidation of the different OO methods is all the rage.

Figure 3–1 shows the object model for a personnel application. In this application, as can be expected, a *person* is at the core. In an object model, the person object can be subtyped into an employee object, which can be further subtyped into hourly and salaried employees. Sets of employees can then be grouped into workgroups, departments, etc.

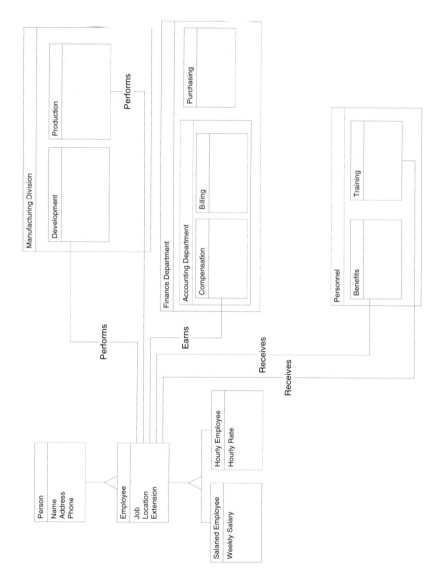

Figure 3–1. Object model for a personnel application.

In a traditional structured (nonobject) model, an entity-relationship diagram is incapable of such feats. Simple sub-typing is allowed, but not the inheritance of functionality from a base class to subclasses. Also, there is no notion of aggregations, such as departments. Transformations must occur between the *ideal* model and the actual implementation of the application that causes a *department* to become a row in an SQL table of *organizations* which must be *joined* in an application to other rows in an *employee* table in order for a *department,* as a user understands it, to be re-created. All of this translation makes it difficult to add features in the future, as the new transformations from new business objects to new structured implementations must be forced to fit on top of the old transformations, as well as add new complexity, etc.

CAPTURING INFORMATION IN OBJECT-ORIENTED BUSINESS SYSTEMS

A key aspect of today's object modeling techniques is their employment of *use cases.* Use cases were pioneered by Ivar Jacobsen and are now used in most of the more prevalent object modeling techniques. Use cases capture how the user interacts with the information system. The user is the *agent,* who generates *input events,* which are then acted upon by the system in a *system operation,* which then generates an *output event.* Use cases are generally created during user interviews as a system is being built and can then be further refined with prototypes that show the user interface on a GUI. This prototype has no back end to it but allows the user to perform interactions on it and see what the results of certain inputs would be.

Once use cases have been developed, the system operations that support those user interfaces can be defined.

Use case scenarios characterize how the system will be used. Next the object and operation models are derived (Figure 3–2). These three activities comprise the Analysis phase. Figure 3–3 shows a simple use case scenario. The billing system is informed by an employee that a product has been shipped to a customer. The billing system sends a bill to the customer, who makes a payment that is entered into the billing system. The billing system then notifies the employee that the product has been paid for. Much more complicated systems can be conceived of and documented with this approach. Figure 3–4 depicts a segment of an information base in the form of an object model. The model shows product information, financial information, and personnel information. The model depicts general-specific information (object inheritance), relationships between objects, and some object attributes.

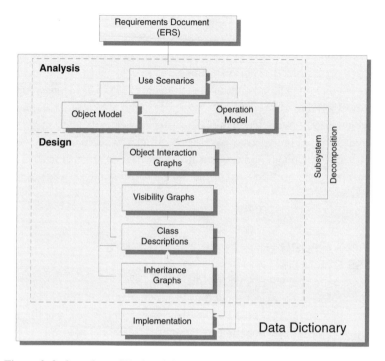

Figure 3–2. Overview of Fusion OO Analysis and Design Method.

The operation model (Figure 3–5) is declarative. That is, it says what the state of the system is prior to an operation, and what the state is after the operation is completed. It gives no indication of how the operation should be performed, which is a design-time activity.

At design time, the operation model becomes a set of Object Interaction Graphs (OIGs). As show in the Figure 3–6, an object interaction graph captures at a detailed level the messages that flow between objects. OIG building is followed by creation of Visibility Graphs, Class Descriptions, and further discovery of inheritance.

MODELING THE DISTRIBUTED ENTERPRISE

The notation and semantics of object modeling tools in general use are similar to what are shown above. Most notations do not account for distributed object development. Booch notation allows for the creation of physical objects such as processors and devices, which can represent distributed systems. Certain toolkits, such as Paradigm Plus, have added extensions dealing with physical entities such as networks, servers, and clients, but these have not yet become standard. Certain groups have added such extensions as concurrency to Fusion, for example, to help with multiple processors, etc.

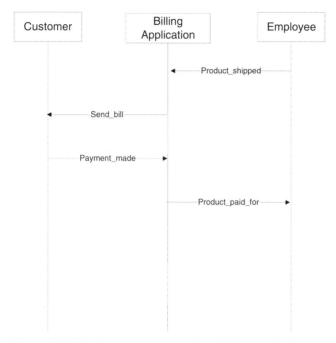

Figure 3–3. Simple use case scenario for a billing application.

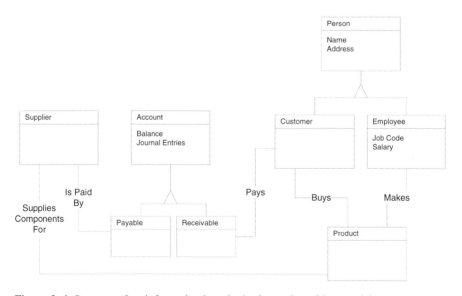

Figure 3–4. Segment of an information base in the form of an object model.

Operation: Product_Purchased

Description: This system operation is invoked by an employee. It informs the billing
              application that a product has been purchased.

Reads: supplied Product_number
         supplied Customer_information
         Product_price

Changes: Customer

Sends: Customer:{Bill}

Assumes: Product_number is valid

Result: Customer_information is added or updated in Customer file.
         Bill is sent to customer.

Figure 3–5. Operation models are declarative. They don't tell how an operation is
performed, only the initial and result states.

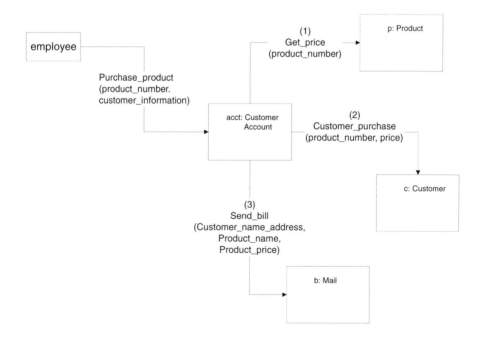

Figure 3–6. The object interaction graph displays message flow between objects.

In general, however, use of object model techniques for concurrency, parallelism, and distribution have not yet been standardized. A great deal of work is going on in this arena, however. For example, Douglas Schmidt of Washington University in St. Louis (http://www.cs.wustl.edu/~schmidt) has discovered several interesting design patterns related to concurrency, parallelism, and distribution. Figure 3–7 shows a framework of patterns that Dr. Schmidt has uncovered. He has implemented these patterns in his Adaptive Communications Environment (ACE) toolkit. More information on both the patterns and the toolkit are available at Dr. Schmidt's Web site.

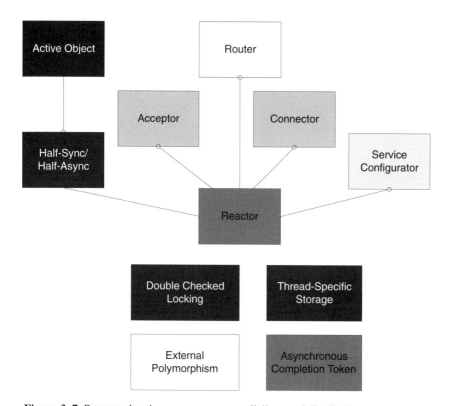

Figure 3–7. Patterns showing concurrency, parallelism, and distribution.

4

OBJECT-ORIENTED CLIENTS

Marshall McLuhan has said that the *medium is the message*. To the end-user, the interface is the machine. Whatever is presented to the user on the display screen is what he thinks of as the information system. The user doesn't want to care about all of the hardware or wiring or software that developers put into such a system. For too long, however, they have had to care about many of those things to be able to use the systems effectively. Object-oriented desktop client workstations (OOClients), enabled by distributed object technology, will help IS professionals go the next step in helping end users ignore the way an information system is implemented.

THE INTERFACE IS THE MACHINE

The first desktop display devices were text and command-line oriented. They were better than punched cards, to be sure, but the user still needed to remember a great deal in order to interact with the system. An MVS *READY* prompt, or an MS-DOS *C:\>* prompt is not particularly helpful in letting the user know how to proceed (Figure 4–1).

This type of system was limited to a few select commands, requiring a user to translate their needs into a stilted verbal form before being able to communicate with the system. To consider how limiting this was, imagine that in order for you to interact with anything in your environment, you needed to type in a command. To open the door to your car, you would need to type *open car door* on the door's keypad. To

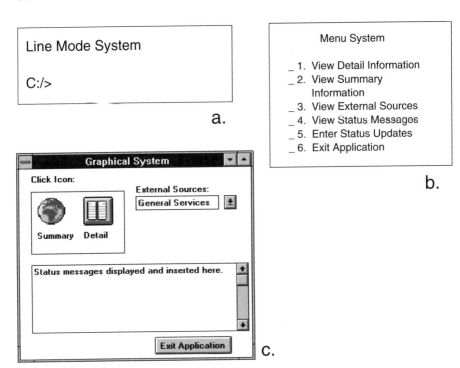

Figure 4–1. Three user interfaces: (a.) Line Mode System, (b.) Menu System, and (c.) Graphical System. The Graphical System generally provides the best usability.

turn the corner, you would type *turn forward wheels 50 degrees to the left.* To open the file drawer at your desk, you would type in *open top desk drawer.* Retrieving a file folder from your desk would require you to name it something with less than eight letters and use that name to refer to it. If you couldn't remember the name of the folder, you would just sit there, looking at a drawer full of file folders, frustrated because you knew it was in there, but you couldn't figure out how to get the system to give it to you.

While these examples are a bit far-fetched, they don't even begin to illustrate the difficulty that we are presented with when faced with trying to use a complex information system with no more help than a blank screen and a cursor. We do not interact with much of our physical environment using a textual interface. To do so would be cumbersome in the extreme. We were accustomed to dealing with information systems in this way, however, but only until something better presented itself.

Menu-oriented systems go far to help a user navigate an information system. They present a list of options that are available in the particular context displayed at that moment (Figure 4–1). They also save on typing. What they don't save on is reading. The user still needs to read and interpret what is displayed. When complex data that doesn't translate into text well are presented to a user, the user is just as likely to be confused as he is to be illuminated. For example, graphs and charts often do a much better job of presenting statistical and numerical relationship data than do numbers in columns. Even navigating around an information system is made easier when the means of navigation is presented graphically, rather than by menus. Menus can't provide visual cues that may quickly alert an end user to the path she may want to take.

Graphical user interfaces go the step beyond textual menu systems. GUIs provide many methods of pictorially representing information (Figure 4–1). Whereas a menu system requires reading, pictures are readily recognized. These interfaces are much more intuitive and easy to use. GUIs may present information in whatever form is most logical. A watch or hourglass indicates the need to wait. Icons with memorable pictures are used to perform actions on word processing documents. Pictures of file folders represent directories that contain documents. Drop-down list boxes reduce screen density (the amount of data on a screen as compared to *white space*) and permit a choice of values to be made (the list boxes can even contain pictures instead of words). A multimedia application presents a window with the look and feel of a tape deck or VCR (without the flashing *12:00*).

With a GUI, even children can easily move about an application. For example, the drawing program Micrografx® Crayola® Art Studio (Figure 4–2) presents a picture of a child's room with coloring books, certificate and badge makers, or an artist's easel as objects spread around the room. To use the coloring book, for example, the child clicks on the picture of a coloring book and is presented with a robust (for a child) but very easy to use graphics tool, primed with coloring book pages and pictures.

However, even graphical user interfaces have their limitations, both for end users and developers. There is currently very little integration of the different kinds of end user tools available on a graphical client. While a single tool may be very powerful, it is difficult to fully integrate information from multiple tools. Each type of information is most readily accessed via its *native* tool. To access documents such as business letters and memos, one uses a word processor. To access graphics documents, one uses a graphics package, and so on. If one wants to embed a graphics item in the word processor, extra work is required, especially if the file is stored in a database or on a remote system. Tools such as cutting and pasting and macro languages simplify the integration, but extra work is still required. While this sort of work is simple for one or two occasions, it quickly becomes cumbersome to continually need to perform such activities every time information needs to be pulled together from different formats.

Figure 4–2. User interface for Micrografx Crayola Art Studio®. As long as a child can understand how the mouse moves the cursor, they can navigate through this type of application.
Source: Micrografx Crayola Art Studio®.

THE SYNERGY OF OBJECTS AND GUIs

Standards in the arena of distributed object technology, such as the Object Management Group (OMG) CORBA, Microsoft's OLE, and more recently, Web browsers and servers, are being developed to simplify integration and usability of multiple GUI applications. They are leading the way for simple GUIs to become Object-Oriented Graphical User Interfaces, or OOGUIs.

OOGUIs go farther than GUIs in that they hide the implementation of data formats and access methods from the user. As in Amy's session in Chapter 1, the user doesn't need to worry about whether something was created in a word processor, a graphics package, or even a child's drawing program. As the user is presented with a compound document (one that contains data from many types of tools), they merely interact with the parts of the document in ways natural to each type of data. If there are tables in the document, the user interacts with them as with spreadsheet data. Behind the scenes, spreadsheet software is activated to interact with the user's inputs. If there are graphical items, whether charts or pictures, the user interacts with them, and the appropriate software is invoked behind the scenes to respond to the user's actions.

OOGUIs enable an intelligent workstation to become an object-oriented client or OOClient when the workstation is integrated with an OOServer and OONetwork. As will be discussed in the following chapters, OOServers and OONetworks work synergistically with OOClients to hide not just the implementation of data (that is, what software is used to access the data) but also to hide the location of the data (where the data is on the network). An OOClient, then, is a OOGUI with location transparency. All data appears local, integrated, and in a more natural format. Compared to its predecessors in the user interface arena, OOClients make data easier to access (fewer worries about word processors, spreadsheet programs, or data access applications), and easier to find (the data is represented in graphical forms that are natural to navigate, like shared filing cabinets, buildings, and offices).

Microsoft's OLE is probably the most important driver for OOClients today. This is not necessarily due to OLE's technical superiority but because of the market share enjoyed by Microsoft operating systems and applications, and OLE's early market availability. Many hundreds of OLE-compliant client and server applications are available today. Most applications and software development tool vendors have developed or are in the process of providing OLE interfaces to their products.

Another trend in client development is the much increased use of desktop applications as components of business applications. Since spreadsheets, word processors, graphics packages, geographic information system packages, and the like are so powerful, an increasing trend is simply to create *applications* that are little more than specialized integrations of these software packages. These *large-grained* component objects may be distributed by various means. The most common means for distributing large-grained objects today is as files, although other means are also possible, such as using OLE interfaces to Oracle relational databases, for example. As OLE becomes more powerful, these large-grained objects will become finer and smaller.

WHO, WHAT, AND WHERE

For an OOClient to be able to access distributed objects, three primary pieces of information are needed. First, the method or function to be invoked needs to be specified. Second, the object to invoke the function against needs to be specified. Third, the host machine that contains the object needs to be specified. Put another way, the question is who, what, and where. Who is the object to be accessed? What is the action to be performed on the object? Where is the object?

From a client perspective, there are many ways to support who, what, and where. (This is the *how.*) With one approach, the client software must interface with a proxy object or application. This proxy object represents the server to the client application. It is responsible for the marshaling of parameters and connecting to the remote machine that will provide the service to the client. This proxy object could contain all the information it needs to perform the function, or it may use other services, such as interface repositories or naming services, to process the request and transmit it to the remote machine.

To the client object, the remote server object appears local. This is the beauty of DOT. It makes the *how* of accessing a remote server object invisible to the client object. The more elegant the DOT technology used, the more flexible the proxy object can be.

The simplest solution is to have a *hard-coded* proxy object. This is a proxy object that is *hard-wired* to a specific server machine and perhaps to a specific server object. As levels of indirection are added, there is more flexibility in the capabilities of the proxy. The proxy may connect to a naming service so that if the server object moves, the proxy doesn't need to be changed. The proxy may use an interface repository so that if the interface to a server object changes, the proxy doesn't need to be changed.

This increased elegance brings with it an increased level of support and programming necessary to use it effectively.

In the technology chapters, the use of proxies will be further explored. In a CORBA implementation, object adapters provide sophisticated access to naming services, object request brokers, etc. With OLE, various implementations of distribution provide everything from hard-coded machine addresses to CORBA-like host resolution services. World Wide Web Uniform Resource Locators typically store the *who*, *what*, and *where* as *what://where/who*, that is, *scheme://machine.domain/full-path-of-file*, or some variant of this.

Today's desktop client systems are destined to become the OOClients of the future. The true value of the client is its ability to provide an effective interface for the user to the rest of the information network. This doesn't diminish the importance of the desktop machine — indeed, it emphasizes it. The personal computer will come into its own as the personal interface to the world.

5

OBJECT-ORIENTED SERVERS

Servers are the workhorses of the distributed object environment. Servers are the places where information is stored and shared. Without servers, a desktop client is just a thin veneer over very limited information. Servers have evolved just as clients have. Servers have gone from being just a place to store raw data in the form of files to highly specialized devices that store data in very complex structures. Servers provide business-specific application services to desktop clients, store any kind of data from simple text to scanned images and audio/video clips, and help a desktop client locate any kind of data anywhere on a network.

DATA WITH CONTEXT

Knowledge workers (which include more of the work force all the time) are being bombarded with greater and more varied types of data all the time. Any aid that will simplify and help organize this data is of benefit to them. It is becoming increasingly important, therefore, to be able to understand what any new information means as quickly and effectively as possible. Information stored in computers can quickly lose its meaning, especially as it is encoded and *massaged*, with the business rules hidden in application programs understood only by its developers. The context of information is the environment the information resides in, how it is used, and what other information relates to it. Another way to refer to *context* as defined here is the *business-object interface*. The more context a user has, or related business information about a piece of data, the more easily a user will be able to decipher and use computer stored information. Indeed, in cognitive psychology, "theorists are beginning to stress an *inextricable* link between contextual constraints and the acquisition of knowledge" (*Context and Cognition: Ways of Learning and Knowing*, Paul Light, et al. eds., L. Erlbaum Associates, Hillsdale, N.J.) That is, the more context available for a new piece of information, the more easily that information will be understood.

For example, in isolation, otherwise easily understood information is meaningless and therefore useless. In Amy's session, for example, much of the information associated with Heather's package would have been more difficult to use had it not all been together in a single *context*. In a paper environment, perhaps the customer's RFP would have arrived in Amy's in tray first. A day later, the outline from Sales would have appeared. Amy would have had to re-create the context in her mind to effectively utilize the outline. Later in the afternoon, the customer's annual report would appear with a cryptic note from Heather, who doesn't have time to properly *place* the annual report in the context it needs to be for Amy to understand its value.

It is not enough to provide a category to provide the full and necessary context for information. Often, in large organizations, a term for a type of information or data item may have several different meanings depending upon the way or place that the information is being used. For example, in a financial institution, the term *loan* may mean many different things. There are fixed rate loans, adjustable rate loans, etc. An Adjustable Rate Mortgage (ARM) may be computed differently depending on the bank. Certain loans may or may not have points associated with them, etc.

In such cases, the only way to fully define what a *loan* is, is by the business rules used in relation to the particular type of loan. These business rules fully define the *behavior* of the loan. The business rules define what information is needed to *create* a loan and what the valid states of that data are, etc. From an OO perspective, the way that these business rules are implemented is in the object's methods.

To further complicate matters, information systems add to the problem of interpreting data. For example, a database filled with financial data is difficult to understand without the *business rules* that give it meaning. Typically these business rules are bound up in the application programs that are used to access the data (Figure 5–1). In order for someone to be able to interpret the data properly, the information needs to be looked at in the context of the business rules coded in the application program.

Business rules hidden in a traditional application program are difficult to integrate in a client/server environment. The rules need to be broken out of the program and attached more effectively to the data in a database to be useful. By associating business rules as closely as possible with the database, you provide more *meaning* to the data. For example, imagine a dictionary that contained only nouns. This would be

```
Typical-Cobol-Module  Pseudo-code
01 Display Screen
02 Manipulate Data  /* hidden business rules */
03 Access Database
04 Display Screen
05 Access Database
06 Interface with Operating System
07 Display Screen
08 Manipulate Data  /* hidden business rules */
09 Display Screen
10 Access Database
11 Manipulate Data   /* hidden business rules */
12 Access Operating System Function
```

Figure 5–1. Programs typically contain business rules mixed in with user interface and database access routines. This intermixing reduces the reusability of the business rules in other applications.

equivalent to giving a user a database without business rules. When verbs (the action words) are included, the dictionary becomes richer and more useful. So it is with a server. An OOServer contains the nouns and the verbs of business — data and business rules, linked closely together.

The result of this tying of business rules with database information is a set of interfaces that are *exported* by the server. These interfaces can be directly accessed by an OOClient and provide a means to more easily access the right information in the right context. When data is *objectified*, a context is given to it in the form of the methods that surround the data. These methods contain the business rules and provide the information with its context.

For example, assume a database containing time series data attached to company identification information (Figure 5–2). This time series data contains calendar dates connected to another series of numbers that always have two decimal places. This data could be stock prices through the day for consecutive dates. The

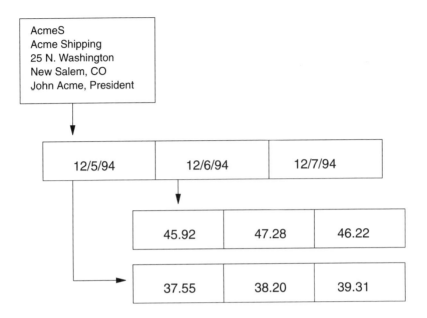

Figure 5–2. Stock time series data.

means to understanding this information is through the metadata attached to the information. This metadata is contained in the names of the data items (objects), as well as the method signatures of the objects. This metadata provides the context for the data (Figure 5–3). For non-object data stores, the only metadata available is the names of the fields. Often, as in the example of the time-series data, this isn't enough to provide the necessary context for understanding the data. The method signatures provide additional context necessary to fully understand how the stored information is to be used.

DATA MODELING THROUGH OBJECTS

Whether application developers do so consciously or not, they model the application systems they develop. Computer-assisted software engineering will be covered in a later chapter, but a brief discussion of the effect of modeling on OOServers is relevant here. An OOServer doesn't just provide *data with context*. It also provides the observer with the ability to understand all of the relationships that surround the information it contains. An OOServer containing information on airline reservations, for example, doesn't need to be limited to the basic interfaces for making a reservation. It can also have information describing links between reservations and the carriers, or links to a carrier's frequent flyer program, and so on.

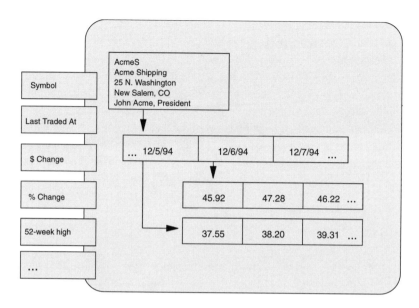

Figure 5–3. The same data encapsulated in a stock object. The interface methods provide extra clues as to how the information can be used and understood.

An OOServer may be browsable, so that a user looking for interfaces can leaf through a list of them under various categories. When a user finds the right server interface, the interface itself may be able to tell the OOClient the right kind of GUI interface to provide for the information.

Data can be stored in servers in several ways. You can use a relational database that has an OO front end, a *pure* OO database, and simple files to store information. There are pros and cons to each approach. Relational databases are most prevalent, and so have more tools and examples of successful implementations. OO Databases have a richer capability set for storing complex objects.

SERVER IMPLEMENTATION

An OOServer doesn't have to be fully object-oriented to be valuable. Far from it. Indeed, OOServers may be legacy systems that have been enhanced to have an OO look and feel to them. This topic will be more fully discussed in Chapter 12, but a brief look is in order here.

The vast majority of today's information is resident in mainframes. The problem is how to access this information effectively. One way is to put a friendlier face on the machine. This may involve the introduction of an additional server machine to provide an OO interface that then translates the OOClient's request into something understood by a COBOL program or an Information Management System (IMS) transaction.

This *three-tier* approach is gaining in popularity. The OOClient connects to an OOServer, which then interfaces to a legacy data source. The communication between the legacy data source may be simple database calls, or may be remote procedure call invocations of application code on the legacy machine. Using RPC invocations may require reworking some of the code on the legacy system but may still be much less work than rewriting the entire legacy system to run in a native fashion on an OOServer.

THE "HOW"

For any OOServer, either *native* or a front end to a legacy system, the important functions are the *how* of data access and retrieval. Since the OOServer is the workhorse of any DOT system, the more the server can do to provide simple-to-use, elegant services to the client, the better. Performance is also a key issue. Correctly implemented object technology can perform much more efficiently and effectively than simple file systems, relational databases, and even a third-generation language business service layer.

Any of the widely accepted OOServer technologies — Web, CORBA, or OLE — provide technology to enable potentially robust OOServer implementations. They each have strengths and weaknesses as OOServer platforms, which will be explored in their respective chapters.

As OOServers become more widely implemented, the *server* will be elevated to its correct place as the *business object repository*. This will lead to unprecedented access to effectively stored and managed business information. Users will find their information systems more useful and Information Technology (IT) managers will find it easier to provide the kinds of information system their users are demanding.

6

OBJECT-ORIENTED NETWORKS

The network is the facility that links desktop clients, workgroup servers, departmental servers, organizational servers, and external servers. While the tendency is to think of the network as the wire between the computers, it is of course much more than that. In today's local area networks and wide area networks, the *network* includes the wires and routing hardware, as well as a great deal of software. This software is responsible for establishing and maintaining connections, routing messages between end nodes, finding servers, enabling management of network-attached devices, as well as providing the various application programming interfaces to the network that developers and their programs expect.

In this sense, the network can be imagined to be expanding outward from the simple wire connecting the devices with the additional facilities mentioned above. This forms the *layers* of the network: physical link, logical link, on up to application level. As more and more components and layers are added to the network, the nature of the network changes. From a developer's and end-user's perspective, the network is simply the interfaces that they use to access the kinds of information that they want.

A developer or end user may view a network as object oriented when it possess some of the characteristics of OO systems. If the *network* supports finding objects by reference, provides location/implementation encapsulation to protect the user/developer from needing to know given objects' locations and implementation platforms, if there is support for inheritance (interface inheritance is especially relevant for network object access), etc., then it is fair to think of the network itself as an object-oriented network (OONetwork). Figure 6–1 shows some of the basic parts of an OONetwork.

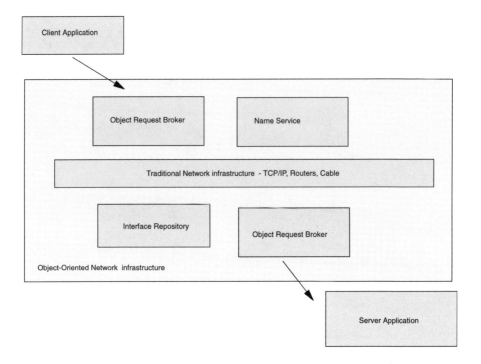

Figure 6–1. The components of an OONetwork.

HYPERSPACE IS HERE

Numerous science fiction books and television shows refer to an almost magical phenomenon in outer space called hyperspace. Through this *space*, ships can travel farther and faster than is possible in normal space. This is the realm where wormholes and warp drive live. While it is unknown whether such things really exist or not, the perception of it may exist for end users when accessing OONetworks.

Indeed, the Web is a prime example of how an OONetwork can function. At one moment, a user is browsing a document on a local server. With a button click, the user is accessing a database on a machine 2,000 miles away. One more click, and the user is downloading a file from a server in another country. This is *moving through hyperspace* in a virtual sense.

Importantly, an OONetwork is not simply an aggregation of OOClients and OOServers. While a single OOClient and OOServer pair may possess between them some of the characteristics mentioned above, as additional OOClients and OOServers are introduced, the need for additional services that are more network oriented becomes apparent. The need for routing object messages between a particular OOClient to a particular OOServer requires software that is not available in most networks today. An object-aware *router* or location broker is needed. This is where the Object Request Broker (ORB) technology standardized by the Object Management Group (OMG) and others such as Hypertext Transfer Protocol (HTTP) with Domain Name Services (DNS) come into play.

ORBs, ORB locators, and CORBAservice name servers on the network act like object-oriented routers and name servers on the network. If an OOClient wants to access a particular object on a particular OOServer somewhere on the network, the ORB and its related services provide the facilities to help locate and route the object request to the OOServer without the OOClient having to worry about it. If the particular OOServer is relocated or otherwise altered, the ORB and its services help protect the client from needing to be changed as well.

The object view is a very powerful way to view the network and its server resources. When a developer/user with his OOClient is empowered to specify *what* they want, without consideration for how to access it or where it is located, they can spend more time doing work related to their business rather than doing work related to the implementation of their information system. Referring again to Amy's session in Chapter 1, she was not required to know where the client information was stored, or where the draft of the business strategy was stored, etc. As far as she was concerned, those items were sitting on her desk.

This is the paradoxical fact about OONetworks. As OONetwork technology improves the ability to place information that a user needs almost anywhere in the world, it also increases the user's sense that the data is right at their fingertips (hence Bill Gates's vision of Information At Your Fingertips or IAYF™).

The World Wide Web is a phenomenon that has grown from the network out. The server components are not particularly well defined — indeed, many Web servers are simply collections of files. The client components are fairly simple — primarily browsers such as Netscape Navigator. The real strength of the Web is its simplicity and ubiquity. URL's hide the complexity of dealing with different types of *logical* servers (HTTP, FTP, Telnet, SMTP, Newsgroups), while the *logical* services, which have been ported to a wide variety of platforms and use TCP/IP as a common network protocol, provide a measure of encapsulation for server implementations. There is a much freer, ad hoc nature to the services available on the Web than with CORBA standards. As people had a need to access documents and various other types of information on many types of platforms, the various foundation technologies of the Web evolved. The technologies of the Web evolved themselves from simple command-line interfaces such as Telnet and FTP to more menu-oriented network interfaces such as gopher and then on to the graphical interfaces of hypertext transfer protocol and hypertext markup language.

Perhaps without realizing it, as the Web network technologies evolved, they also became more object based. A URL is essentially a distributed object reference. It holds information on the location of an *object*, the operation to perform on the object, and the *name* of the object itself. Web technologies will gradually adopt some of the kinds of services used in CORBA. They may end up looking different in the Web implementation, but the need is still there for them. To a large degree, CORBA predicts the evolution of the Web, the most pervasive OONetwork in place today.

7

OBJECT-ORIENTED
INTEGRATION

Distributed object technology consists of three key pieces: OOClients, OOServers, and OONetworks. The interaction of these components provides the synergy that makes up DOT. OOClients alone, as was previously stated, do not make a distributed object network. The question may be asked: In what form does this synergy happen? What are it benefits? Why is it worth the expense to put all of these elements in place? This chapter will deal with these types of questions.

ENCAPSULATION: MAKING THE PIECES FIT (THE DEVELOPER'S VIEW)

Encapsulation provides information hiding in which independent software units protect themselves by hiding the internal details from the outside world (*Distributed Computing*, Raman Khana, ed., Prentice Hall, 1994). This is important to information systems developers because it enables them to change distributed object systems component by component without having to rewire the entire system.

For example, assume a DOT system in a large manufacturing organization. This system keeps track of new orders, the status of the orders, and shipment information. It is distributed from the executive office, throughout management, and on the plant floor (Figure 7–1). As with any other information system, this one will periodically need enhancements. As a new enhancement, say red-flagging any order that hasn't been filled within five days, is needed, it can be implemented on an OOServer as soon as the server developers are finished with it. Due to

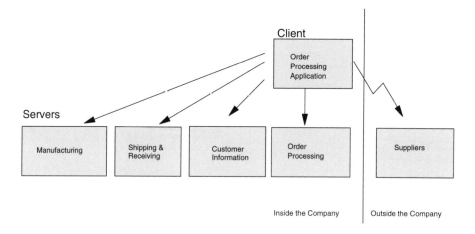

Figure 7–1. DOT system for a manufacturing organization.

encapsulation of the service as a new method call on the server, the OOClient doesn't need to be aware of the service the moment it is implemented. The client developers can then take advantage of it whenever they want. There is no need for coordination on the part of the server developers with the client developers. When the client developers want to make the new functionality available to the end user, they simply add the method call to their client and make the interface available to the end user.

Additionally, if a new OOServer is added to the network, its services may be made available to the OOClient transparently, without the other OOServers needing to be altered in any way. The OONetwork via the object request broker handles making new servers available to clients in a flexible, dynamic way. Indeed, an OOServer may in fact be an OOClient accessing other OOServers and then performing a higher-level function on the information before passing it on to the desktop OOClient. For example, a decision support system may be implemented on an OOServer that makes requests of many OOServers already on the network prior to aggregating the results and giving them back to the OOClient on a user's desk (Figure 7–2).

SEAMLESS OBJECTS FROM YOUR DESKTOP
TO MINE (THE USER'S VIEW)

The synergy of OOClients, OOServers, and OONetworks, while beneficial to developers, is more important for its impact on end users' productivity. When an information system automates the simple tasks that an end user needs to perform, it is paying for itself. When it simplifies the difficult tasks that an end user needs to perform, it is returning significant dividends.

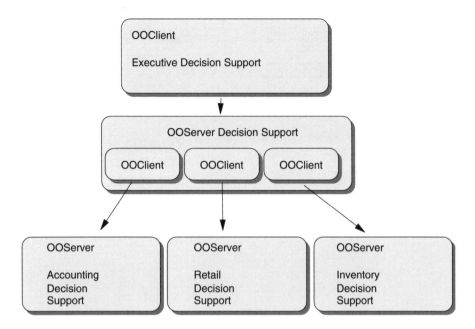

Figure 7–2. DOT-enhanced decision support system.

For example, assume again the large manufacturing company. In Figure 7–3 is an illustration of what a typical order status screen might look like. It has most of the relevant information about the order. What it doesn't have is all of the other information that a user of that screen might want. What if someone calls and asks what the ordered item looks like? What if someone wants to know what other parts might be substituted for the ordered item? What about finding out where, exactly, in the production run the ordered item is located (has the work on the order actually been begun, or is the item still in an input queue somewhere?).

What if the order is for a custom part that perhaps has complicated specifications? How can these be accessed? What if the order is for a product that is the result of many components, some of which are supplied by outside vendors? If there is a delay in assembling of the product and one of the outside suppliers is unable to meet demand, how does one find an alternate?

Today, a typical Order Processing (OP) *clerk* is certainly not capable of answering most, if any, of the above questions, especially given the type of information available in a typical order processing application. Any follow-up would need to be done by calling other people, some whose existence the OP clerk doesn't know how to get a hold of and others whose existence the OP clerk isn't even aware of. What if, however, due to the company's use of DOT, an OP clerk was able to *hyperlink* from the order to whatever information source is relevant to answer each

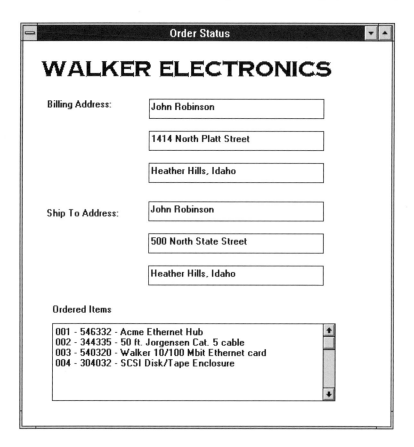

Figure 7–3. Order status screen. This interface doesn't help to navigate to other information sources that can help the user perform their job more effectively. Links to other information sources from the user interface would be helpful.

of the questions above? Figure 7–4 shows a DOT system depicting links from the OP system to various other manufacturing organization systems that enable the *clerk* to become a full-fledged *order manager.* This is accomplished via the developers of the OP system taking advantage of interfaces to other plant systems to acquire the information needed and linking these interfaces to the OP clerk's OOClient in appropriate ways.

This sort of integration of services is a requirement in almost any customer-interaction support system, whether it be order processing, technical response centers, credit card call centers, etc. It is also a need in almost every area where a worker needs information from other areas of the company (which generally means everyone).

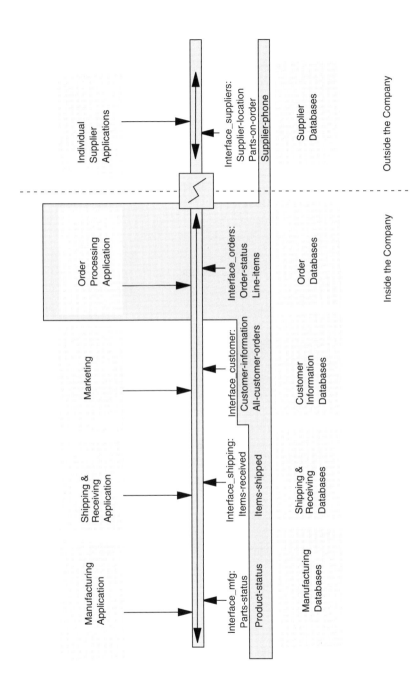

Figure 7-4. This order processing application has links to other systems in the organization. An interface based on this system could allow the user to access almost any information about the order that the customer might request.

A key point here is that the developers of the OP system didn't need to develop special interfaces to get to the information available in the other systems. By building their systems using OOClients and OOServers, the developers of the other plant systems made their systems available to other *users* of the information with no extra effort. In addition, since the only way to access the other plant systems is via OOServer method calls, the OP developers are insulated from future changes to the internal data formats or business rules.

DOT shows its power in this instance as well. As requests are made by either the OOClient or an OOServer to another OOServer, the proxy objects encapsulate the location of the OOServer. That is, if a service interface on an OOServer migrates to another OOServer (physical device), the OONetwork transparently reroutes the service requests from the client to the appropriate server. Furthermore, if a particular service interface is split into multiple interfaces, the OONetwork protects the clients from having to be aware of that fact.

For example, take the order processing application again. Assume that as the application was first written, the order tracking and shipment tracking functions were combined. Now an enhancement request comes in to do more work on the shipment tracking side, perhaps by linking directly in with the computer systems of the external shipping vendors, such as FedEx or UPS. It might be determined at this point that the best implementation for this enhancement is to start from the interfaces provided by FedEx and UPS and build the additional local shipment tracking application code around them. This would necessitate splitting the existing application, separating the order tracking functions from the shipment tracking functions. In the new implementation, the order tracking functions are localized in one OOServer, while the shipment tracking functions are integrated with the encapsulated external vendor interfaces in a different OOServer. The OONetwork makes this change opaque to OOClients (Figure 7–5). All the OOClients see is the new service interfaces that are available (such as being able to find out where, exactly, a shipped product in transit is currently located) due to the encapsulated external vendor interfaces.

Certainly, these types of changes could have been developed and implemented with existing, structured development techniques. The difference here is one of degree. The use of DOT, primarily data/function and location encapsulation, reduces the amount of software development work required to implement this sort of application integration.

OOClients provide the interface to objects, OOServers provide for the storage of objects, and OONetworks provide location and routing services to link the two. When all three are combined, the features of object technology — encapsulation, polymorphism, and inheritance — are spread out from a single computer to groups of clients and servers on a network. The results are easier application integration, better reuse of business objects and services, and easier-to-use information systems.

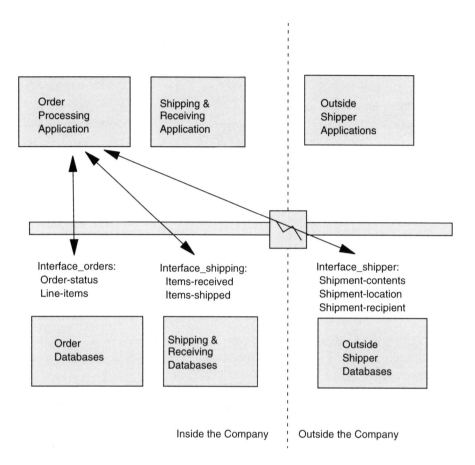

Figure 7–5. A DOT system can access interfaces inside or outside the company. Internally developed server applications may be replaced with externally provided applications with reduced impact on the client application and user interface.

BUILDING BLOCKS

This section will discuss some of the component objects (building blocks) that were used in applications Amy used in the scenario in Chapter 1. It will show the types of objects that need to be created and how they integrate to form applications for end users.

At the bottom level are basic objects that can be reused to build more complex objects. These first objects are technology oriented: containers, video objects, voice objects, text objects, spreadsheet objects, etc. They have little value of themselves but are very powerful when put together in various configurations. They are depicted in Figure 7–6.

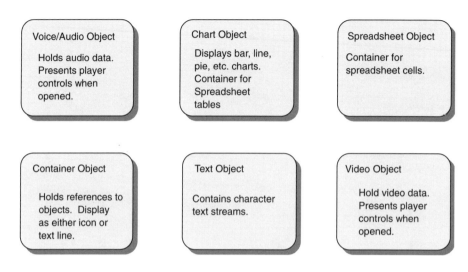

Figure 7–6. Technology objects.

At the next level are business objects. There is an e-mail object. It contains a distribution list and one or more attachments. The distribution list is actually a list of person objects that shows only a *view* of the names of the people on the list. If a user opened a distribution list and clicked on a person's name, the publicly available *business card* of that person would be shown.

A business card is another business object. An in tray and an out tray are business objects. They are container objects that are associated with an owner (a person), as well as a set of objects that can be put in an in tray (such as e-mails or anything else that might be normally dropped in a person's in tray). Figure 7–7 shows these objects.

Amy has *magazine* objects in her in tray. A magazine is a container object that contains articles and advertisements. An article is a series of text and graphics and picture (and video) objects that may well just be *views* into other, more complete objects. An advertisement is also a series of text and graphics and picture objects. Articles and advertisements may actually be subclasses/specializations of a *compound view object* (Figure 7–8). This compound view object is just an object of any sort that may contain text, graphics, etc. An article object may be subclassed and contain other information, such as the author, reference links, etc., while an advertisement object may be limited to a certain length and contain information such as cost, number of times it is viewed, etc.

Amy has a several voice mails in her in tray. These are sound objects that contain an audio stream, along with envelope information (caller name, time sent, length, etc.) The sound objects also contain text information that came from interpreting the

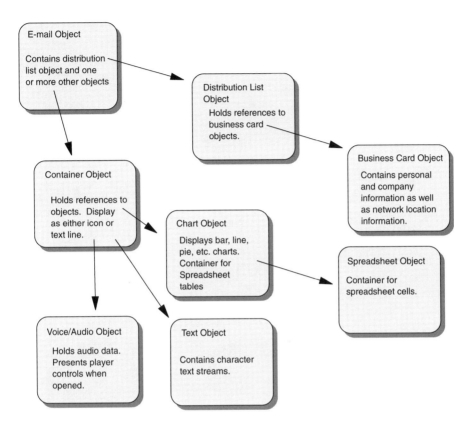

Figure 7–7. Business object made up of technology component objects.

voice message into text. Therefore, the voice mails are containers that contain the audio stream, the envelope information, and the textual translation of the message.

There is a video conference object that contains the *minutes* of a meeting Amy missed. It is a container object that has a video stream from the coordinator's view, the notes taken by the coordinator of the meeting, and attachments of the relevant background material for the meeting.

The draft outline created by Heather in Sales is a type of container object. The outline is text that is followed by *views* of other objects that are dragged in to the object. These views are either other text objects or other compound objects.

The annual report object is a very interesting one. It is a container object that has events linking the three primary objects together (the video, the text narrative, and the graphics object). It is also interesting in that the graphics object is the same object all the way through. What changes about the object is that as the video progresses, different spreadsheet table objects are linked into the graph object and the

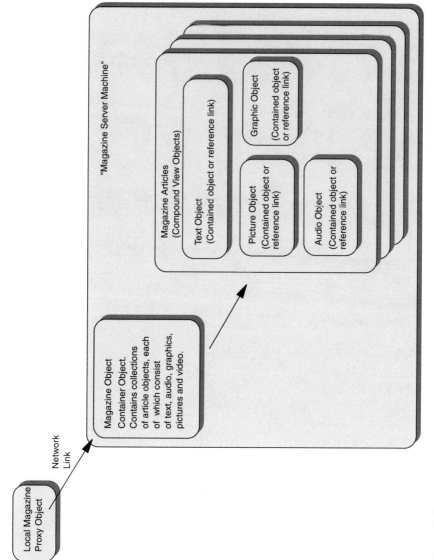

Figure 7–8. Compound view object accessed via a proxy object.

view of the graph is changed (Figure 7–9). This again shows the power of object technology, where a single object can be linked to other objects in sequence that make it appear that the object (this time, the chart) is actually many different objects being presented in sequence.

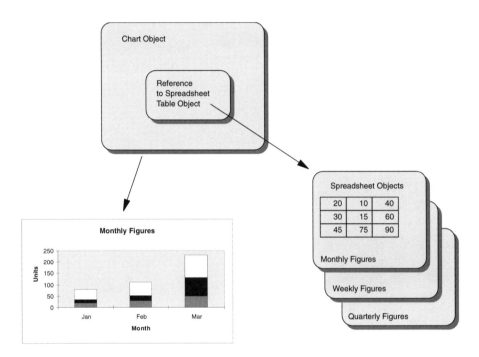

Figure 7–9. Chart object provides a view of a spreadsheet object. A single chart object may appear to be a succession of different chart objects. In fact, different spreadsheet objects are successively linked to the chart object.

8

ENTERPRISE *VIEWS*

In most larger companies, there are separate information systems applications for accessing the company's various databases. There are databases for personnel information accessed by personnel applications. There are financial databases accessed by financial applications. The product databases are accessed by product applications. The sales databases are accessed by sales applications, and so on. These databases and their respective applications represent vertical slices of the company's information base (Figure 8–1).

When a user in Accounting needs access to personnel information, the user either accesses the personnel data via the personnel applications, or makes a request to the information systems department to create or enhance an application to permit access to the personnel databases (Figure 8–2). While this approach works, it does inhibit effective access to company information. It would be better if the IS department were able to provide components (miniapplications) that were accessible to either end users or IS component assemblers to facilitate building of applications that were easy to build. These applications could have the additional benefit of providing links between and within business domains. Figure 8–3 shows how a company's information systems could be architected if components were created to provide access to the company's various databases and were assembled in various ways to provide for effective access based on classes of users' or individual user's needs. Some components, such as technical specifications and marketing plans in Figure 8–3, are shared by multiple end-user applications. To provide such an infrastructure, the IS department would need to develop an enterprise model of the company's applications needs, based on user input and the existing business applications and databases.

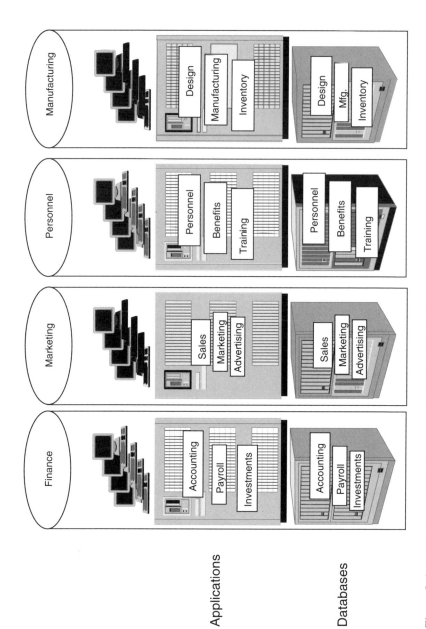

Figure 8–1. Applications and databases are often built within business area silos. It can be difficult later to attempt to share data and functions between them.

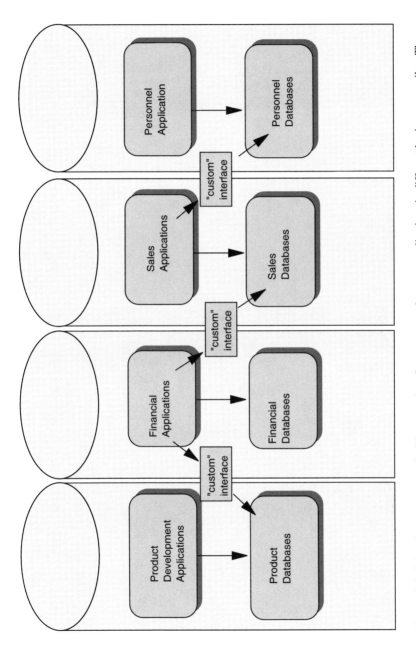

Figure 8–2. It is often necessary to build custom interface programs between applications in different business area silos. These custom programs become extra work to maintain.

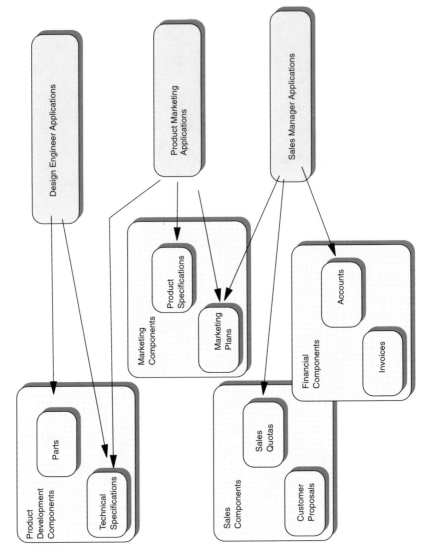

Figure 8–3. A component approach to applications development.

This enterprise model starts out with the most basic objects at the foundation (of which there are probably only a few for many organizations) and builds from there.

For a manufacturing firm, for example, some of the most basic objects may be just product, supplier, division, and customer. Many of the higher-level objects would be built upon these and have some level of specialization.

As the objects become more specialized, different people have different interests in them. This is where views come in. While most people in the company are interested in products and customers in general, there are only a few interested in certain specific products and selected customers. As these people need to combine certain types of information from various sources, they are creating their particular views of the company (Figure 8–4). Historically, the only way to solve the problem of integration is with custom interfaces.

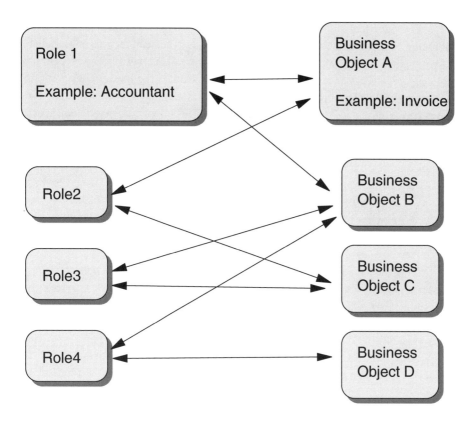

Figure 8–4. People in different roles have varying views of the business objects that make up an organization's information base.

With DOT at our disposal, however, it is now possible to create an infrastructure for the corporation that allows one application area to create objects that are reusable by another application area. These *business objects* represent the business entities and rules that provide the information foundation for the company.

The way these business objects are integrated at the desktop or user level is what makes them valuable. Look at it from a paper perspective. In any company there are numerous forms and reports. Each of these forms and reports generally has numerous people in different roles who are interested in them. Therefore, we have a *many-to-many* relationship. Each form is of interest to many different people and each person has an interest in many different kinds of forms. The contents of the desk of an accountant is different than the contents of the desk of a purchasing agent, which is different than a company lawyer, a shipping manager, etc.

Consider that each of these people have a file on a vendor called Charter Shipping. The file in the accountant's desk will have financial records and a balance of payments sheet for the customer. The purchasing agent has all of the recent purchasing agreements as well as invoices from the vendor. The lawyer has purchasing agreements as well as any relevant legal matters relating to the vendor, such as court cases involving the vendor and other customers. The shipping manager has invoices and recent shipment records for the vendor.

All of the files are different, but many share common *objects.* If we were to automate all of the paperwork for dealing with vendors such as Charter Shipping, we would begin by building base objects such as *Vendor Information, Contracts, Invoices, Shipments, Litigation*, and the like. We would build each of the *files* used by the employees by combining these base business objects in various ways. This process of aggregation or *containment* supports the *view* that each of the employees has of the business relationship with Charter Shipping.

This mechanism of custom aggregation of business objects into appropriate views is nearly universal. That is, it applies to most businesses. All business information is organized in this fashion. Any business other than very small ones needs to share information in complex fashions. Base business objects are built into aggregate view objects that are customized for each employee role.

This is not to say that there is only one level of business object. Indeed, there may be many levels of business objects. At the bottom of a retail object model, for example, are objects such as customer, vendor/supplier, channel/outlet, inventory, personnel, sale, etc. At a higher level may be business customer, consumer customer, preferred supplier, direct channel, indirect channel, warehouse inventory, etc.

While each of these higher-level objects is a specialization of the base business objects, they are also *views* of the base objects. Figure 8–5 shows the relationship between base business objects, derived business objects, and the eventual users. As can be seen, there can be quite an array of relationships, even with just a few objects.

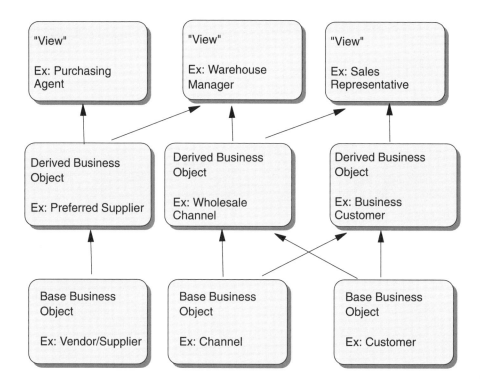

Figure 8–5. Business objects are often derived into more specialized objects.

Distributed object technology provides support for mapping base business objects to different enterprise views. Via subclassing of objects and inheritance of methods and attributes, object technology facilitates creation of derived objects. Object technology also enables creation of *views* of business objects that pull information from multiple-derived objects together into a single view. DOT helps here in that many of these business objects may actually reside on different servers spread throughout the enterprise. DOT helps provide a *single-system* view of this distribution, without removing the benefit that object technology brings.

Part III

Application and Technology

This section contains three chapters that will discuss applications of DOT. There are chapters with focus on CORBA, OLE, and Web technologies. The chapters are designed to give a flavor of how these technologies can be applied to help support the kinds of business and application environments discussed in the previous sections.

In Chapter 9, most of the CORBA concepts will be explained using Distributed Smalltalk (DST). This is an appropriate vehicle because DST is OMG CORBA and CORBAservice compliant because it supports higher-level compound document interfaces in a distributed manner and it is an excellent teaching tool due to its pure object structure.

> Smalltalk...is the programming system that most consistently adheres to the object-oriented paradigm and has served both as a model for object-oriented extensions to existing languages and as the basis for a new generation of languages..." (*Inside Smalltalk,* Wilf R. LaLonde and John R. Pugh, Prentice Hall, 1990.)

Smalltalk is also effective as a learning tool because of the ability to browse code and inspect internal data structures very easily, something not done as easily with C++. In fact, with DST, it is possible to easily inspect data/object structures on a remote machine. Numerous examples will follow that will use these Smalltalk tools. Object persistence and query are explained using examples from Odapter, which is an OO front end to Relational dabases. This brief departure from CORBAservices is due to the desire to show an integrated OO query/persistence mechanism that is available today and is robust enough to use at an enterprise level.

Microsoft Visual Basic will be used to show how tools that haven't traditionally been considered object oriented can utilize distributed objects. Visual Basic supports seamless interfaces for OLE clients and servers. Microsoft has made a small but good start toward distributed object technology, with the introduction of OLE remote automation. Other vendors have also shown how Visual Basic can support OLE over a network, such as Next's PDO and Iona's Orbix.

Netscape Navigator will be used to show how Web technologies are beginning to become more distributed object oriented. Navigator's inclusion of frames and plug-ins, as well as advances on the server side, show that Web technologies are beginning to adopt the kinds of technologies already depended on in OLE and especially in CORBA.

9

ENTERPRISE OBJECTS: CORBA AND CORBASERVICES

This chapter presents an implementation of DOT as defined by the Object Management Group (OMG) in its various CORBA specifications. The specifications dealt with in this chapter are CORBA 1.0, 2.0, and CORBAservices. The example vehicle for explaining CORBA is VisualWorks Smalltalk and the class libraries that support CORBA implementation in that environment — Distributed Smalltalk. CORBA is a technically robust DOT framework.

The genesis of the CORBA work started in 1989 when Hewlett-Packard and eight other companies founded the OMG as an independent organization. At that time, according to Cliff Reeves of IBM, the OMG was basically a *NewWave* admiration society. NewWave was a desktop-oriented, object-based environment developed by Hewlett-Packard. NewWave's purpose was to allow seamless integration of applications on the desktop. NewWave itself, despite heroic efforts on the part of various lab and marketing teams, never found its niche. However, it has spawned numerous progeny, Distributed Smalltalk among them. Windows 95, it might be added, has much of the feel of NewWave.

This chapter will discuss most of the more well developed CORBAservice and CORBA interfaces and operations. It will not go into great depth, which would take a volume many times thicker than this. The intent here is to give the reader a basic feel for the kind of capabilities that exist with CORBA-based DOT and some ways to make use of it. The DOT technologies in the following chapters — OLE and Web technologies — are already pervasive and growing. CORBA is growing in acceptance, especially by the major systems' vendors, and appears to have great promise for enterprise-level applications.

Figure 9–1 provides a visual depiction of the various CORBA components and services. At the foundation of CORBA is the interface definition language and the object request broker. The concept of interface when dealing with objects, either local or distributed, is key, as was mentioned earlier in the book. Object request brokers are essential for hiding the remote implementation of objects that appear local.

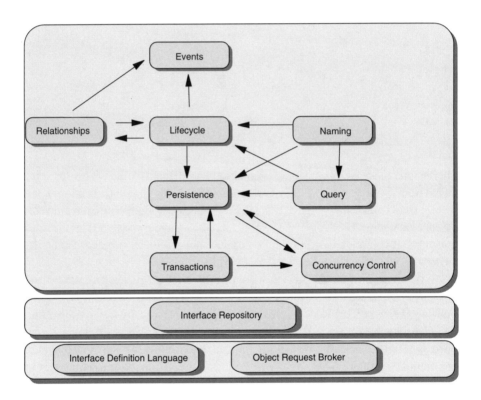

Figure 9–1. A schematic of the key components of CORBA and some of the CORBAservices. Many of the services have dependencies on other services. For example, the naming service may be dependent on the lifecycle, persistence, and query services.

On top of the more basic components is the interface repository (IR). The IR is the place to store and find interfaces that are needed for remote access. Above the IR are the various services that can be used. It is possible to use just the more basic CORBA components without the services to develop distributed object applications. It is the services, however, which bring increased ease of development to the DOT arena, especially in the interoperability arena.

The arrows between the various services depict optional use relationships. That is, for example, that an Event service may use Relationship and Lifecycle services to perform more effectively. A Query Service may benefit from the availability of a Naming service, as do Lifecycle and Persistence services. Each of the services could be developed and deployed exclusive of the other services, but there is a measure of synergy when the various services are developed to depend on one another.

CREATING OBJECTS (LIFECYCLE)

DOT starts with object creation. Once objects have been created, they can be copied, moved, or removed.

All objects have a life cycle. They must be created by some one or some process. They can then be activated and deactivated (attached to a running process on a machine) and they can be moved, copied, and removed. Objects are like elements; some, like gold and lead, are durable and basically permanent — like objects that contain scientific reference information, for example. Other objects are very short-lived, with lifetimes measured in milliseconds — for example, transitory run-time objects that are needed only for the life of a simple transaction.

The most fundamental action on an object is its creation. The creation of an object involves the use of some sort of a *factory* mechanism. A factory is, simply, a manufacturing facility for an object. In the sense that an object can be simple or complex, the manufacturing process for such an object will be similarly simple or complex. A factory hides the process from the client requesting object. This concept may appear new to programmers but is effectively what happens in, for example, relational databases when a row is *INSERTed* into a table.

After an object is developed, it is registered with an object factory. The factory knows how to build an object of a given type and pass the reference to the instance it creates back to the developer's code for his use. From a user perspective, this is similar to opening a drawer and taking out a particular form. This form has an outline of the kind of information it can hold but is blank. For a developer, this is similar to creating a data structure that has a certain format but is empty. The factory allocates the memory for the object and passes the pointer address for the memory back to the requesting object. In Smalltalk, a factory is similar to executing a *new* operator on a certain object class. In C++, a factory is similar to *constructing* an object of a certain class, also with *new*.

The creation process is more than just providing a template, however. The object may have a few or very many default attributes. For example, a folder object may be instantiated but have very little *state* — few properties that have been pre-loaded. A *house* object, however, may be created by an object factory and have very many default attributes and components already established at creation time.

The value of a CORBAservice factory is that it can, for example, create a Smalltalk object on system A on behalf of a C++ object on system B (Figure 9–2). The Smalltalk object could also be on the same system, but in a different address space than the C++ object. Even if both objects are Smalltalk objects or C++ objects on the same machine, the value of a factory is that the object creation interface is standard. Any language or service that understands the CORBA factory protocol can create an object.

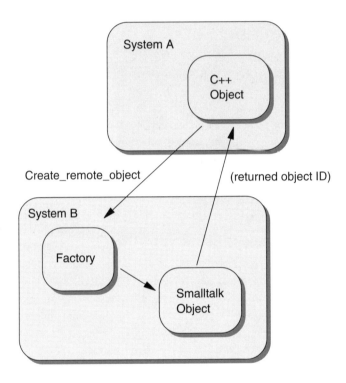

Figure 9–2. A C++ object on System A can use a Factory to create a Smalltalk object on System B.

The created objects can be large or small, simple or complex. A central patient monitoring system can create a small measurement object inside of a heart arrhythmia monitoring application. On the large size, the created object could be an explosion of all the parts typically needed for an automobile, with the factory simply returning a handle to the *automobile object*.

From a user's perspective, the usage model for object factories is fairly simple. As shown in Figure 9–3 in this sample Distributed Smalltalk application, a user

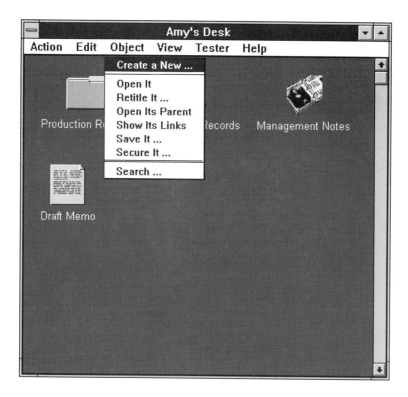

Figure 9–3. Creating a new object using a pull-down selection.

clicks on the Object menu and then the *Create a New* pull-down selection. This results in a dialog box that lists all the available objects to the user. To create a text object, for example, the user selects the text item. A text object is then created and placed in the window of the currently open folder. In order to create a remote object, the user could first navigate a desktop on the chosen remote machine and perform the *Create a New* there (Figure 9–4).

Some sample code for building an object in Distributed Smalltalk is shown in Figure 9–5. Please note that the object created is a distributed object and can be accessed by an application running on a remote machine. The steps involve accessing the object factory (factory finder) using the naming service. Then the factory finder creates the object and passes back a reference to it (*remTextObj*). Once the reference (which is a distributed object reference) is received, it can be acted upon. In this case, we are opening a presentation (or client) object to display the state of the remote object on the local machine's monitor.

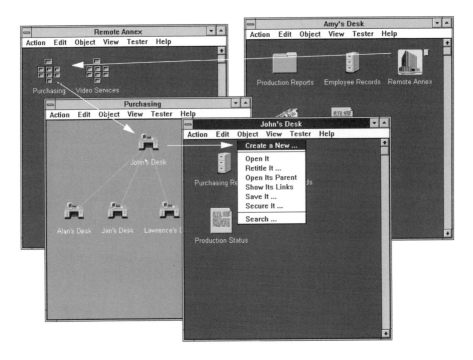

Figure 9–4. Navigating to another *desktop* to create an object.

FINDING OBJECTS (NAMING AND RELATIONSHIPS)

One of the most important pieces of information about a document or a data item or any type of data stored in an information retrieval system is its name. Quite simply, if we can't remember what we named something when we put it away, it's more difficult to find it when we need it!

Every bit of data in a computer system is accessed by its name. For the application programmer, it is the identifier in the program code; for the system administrator, it is the resource name in a configuration tool; for the end user, the name is anything from the file name in Microsoft Word to the table name in a database or the screen name in an application with a certain name (if I could just remember where I put that...).

It was difficult enough to find things when there was very limited information available on the system, in the days when the mainframe was the sole repository of data. Today, with information stored anywhere from your palmtop or laptop to your local desktop machine or local server (or servers), then on to servers in Atlanta,

```
"Declare the local variables"
| ns ffinder remTextObj localPresentationObject |

"Access name server on remote host."
ns := (ORBObject namingService).

"Using name server, access object factory on remote host."
ffinder := ns contextResolve: (DSTName onString: 'owlFactoryFinder').

"Using object factory, create text object on remote host. Give it a title."
remTextObj := ffinder createObject: TextSO getInstanceACL.
remTextObj title: 'Text Object on a remote machine'.

"(Optional) Create a local presentation object to display the remote semantic."
localPresentationObject := remTextObj
        createPresentation: nil
        types: #()
        session: Session
        access: #'read_write'
        auto: true.

"Attach a display window to the local presentation object."
localPresentationObject attachWindow: Session.
```

Figure 9–5. Building a remote object in Distributed Smalltalk.

Seattle, or any other remote site, what you name something (which involves where you put it) is very serious business indeed. This, of course, is complicated by the fact that often the information you are looking for was actually put away by someone else: "I think I put it on the *I:* drive on the Accounting Department server in the PUBLIC subdirectory. On second thought, it may still be on my *C:* drive. I think I also put it on a floppy that I gave to Jeff, too, though."

Transactional, structured information, such as bank account information or payroll information or what have you, is generally easier to find. However, that's really only because traditionally structured information is very limited. You can get your payroll information by calling personnel, but if you want to check on the costs of benefits, such as increased life insurance costs, it may well be that such information is not available to the person handling the transaction. As for managers, executives, and their staffs, it has taken the information warehouse boom to really free such information from its hiding places to be more readily accessible to the people who need to know what is out there in all of those operational databases.

With workgroup members often scattered about the country, being able to label documents and other types of workgroup and enterprise information in such a way as to be easily found is an important matter. The capabilities of the facility that is provided to give the appropriate name to something is important as well. With the CORBAservice naming service, an effort was made to define a standard that is general enough to be widely useful but also detailed enough to be robust in its handling of even large amounts of names and namespaces.

As stated previously, the context of a piece of information is a very important indicator of its usefulness and applicability to the problem at hand. For example, if one were looking for the home address of an employee, they wouldn't look in the company phone directory, which would likely only contain the business address. The meaning of *address* is quite the same in both places, but the added context of *business* versus *home* is what indicates the appropriateness of the address to the current query.

The naming service uses the concept of naming graphs to provide trees of nodes of naming contexts (Figure 9–6). What this means it that to find information, a user would start at some sort of base naming context, perhaps that of their local server. From there, they could navigate to subcontexts that would lead to the actual object they need. In addition, for a developer, trees and graphs of naming contexts provide a tool for storing *labeling* information in the most *realistic* form, not limited by file systems, database systems, or networks.

File systems are limited in that they typically store only aggregate level information, plus there is no optimization for queries of file system data. Databases, especially relational databases, but even object databases, still have the limitation of location in naming and locating information. Relational queries, for example, do not typically find information located in a standard file system on a remote server, nor do they access information that is present in transitory form in a running program on a remote server. Today, it is generally up to the application programmer to navigate the network using the right subsystem (file system, RPC, or interprocess communication (IPC) database query) to find a given data item or object. With a more general naming service, implementations that cross file, database, process, and network boundaries may be accessed from a unified set of interfaces.

There is another element in object naming, which is *granularity*. An Excel spreadsheet is an *object*. It has function and data. It is a large-grained object — at the application level. An Excel spreadsheet cell is also an object, one that is very small or fine-grained, like a name field in a personnel or customer application.

The more fine-grained a set of objects are, the more a naming service is stressed to access them. It is safe to say that at this point, accessing large numbers of very fine

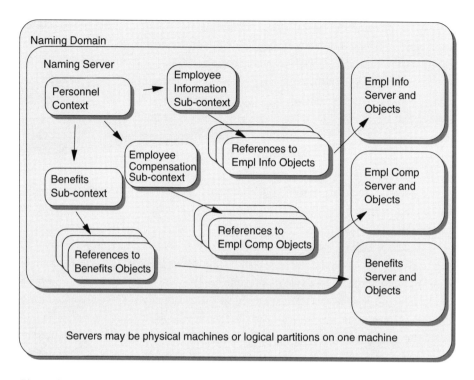

Figure 9–6. Naming Domain containing a Naming Server, Contexts, and Subcontexts. The *leaf nodes* point to objects.

grained objects remains the province of databases. It is not that the CORBAservice naming service interface could not support such applications; rather, it is that the sort of implementation engines that are present today in databases are likely the only ones robust enough to handle the scalability problem of billions or trillions of objects in a single namespace.

The naming service enables a developer to provide various means to allow a user to name and categorize single objects or groups of objects. For example, assume a company has as a base object the *employee* object. This object contains basic information about an employee, such as name, address, phone, etc. In order to group and later locate employee objects, a *Personnel Naming Context* is created. A naming context is basically just a grouping of any kinds of information that you might want to keep together. In the Personnel Naming Context, a sub-context is created called the *Employee Information Naming Context*. As you can see, a naming context can be nested within another naming context.

Next, under the Employee Information Naming Context, we begin to link in Employee Information objects as they are created. Assuming that three Employee Information Objects have been created, the overall picture looks like Figure 9–7. The figure shows Smalltalk *inspectors* opened on a series of objects. The topmost object is ORBObject. ORBObject is the root object for any given DST image or session instance. The ORBObject is an imagewide global object that both provides distributed object functionality to all the objects that inherit from its class as well as a place to store all of the *systemwide* information that needs to be accessed by distributed objects residing on or off the system. The naming service for the image is an attribute of the ORBObject. The next level down is the context for Personnel, then Employee Information, with the actual objects to be found at the bottom.

Figure 9–8 illustrates the code needed to initially create naming contexts as well as to create and bind an object in the namespace. The first thing to be done is to get a *handle* to the naming service for the server. In this instance, we are accessing the name service via an IOR handle from a file. The inter-ORB reference (IOR) was exported from the name service to the file previously.

The next statements traverse down the chain of naming contexts until getting to the base objects. A DSTName is a class of objects that is used by naming contexts. The *bindNewContext:* method creates a new context under the naming context and labels it as *Personnel context.* This context can be retrieved later by using this string. Since contexts can be nested, the next step is to create a new context called *Employee Information Context.* It is bound under the Personnel Context by sending the *bind-NewContext* message to the handle for Personnel's context that was just created.

The next step is to create objects that will reside in these contexts. First, we get a handle to the factoryFinder by sending the appropriate method to the ORBObject. The factoryFinder keeps track of the information needed to create a new object. The createObject method then creates a EmployeeInformationSO. The *getInstanceACL* method returns the abstractClassID for the type of object to be created. The abstractClassID is a Universal Unique Identifier (UUID) that is created specifically for the particular class. It should be the same for that type of class on any system at any time.

The createPresentation method at the end of Figure 9–8 displays the window shown in Figure 9–9. Data in the window was entered manually. Figure 9–10 shows Smalltalk inspectors opened on both the local presentation object and the remote semantic object for the employee information object. Notice that the objectid for the remote semantic matches the DSTObjRefRemote object that is its proxy on the local machine.

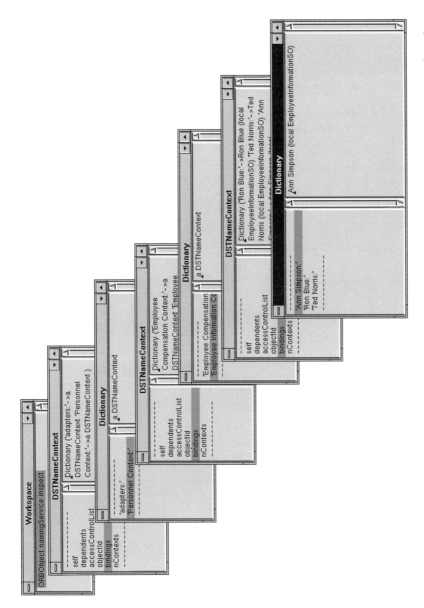

Figure 9–7. Smalltalk inspectors starting at a base *ORBObject* and following links through a name service and naming contexts to individual objects.

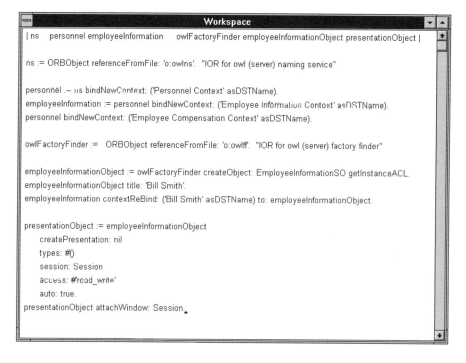

Figure 9–8. Smalltalk code to create a naming context and bind an object to it.

Figure 9–9. Window displayed by createPresentation method of Figure 9–8.

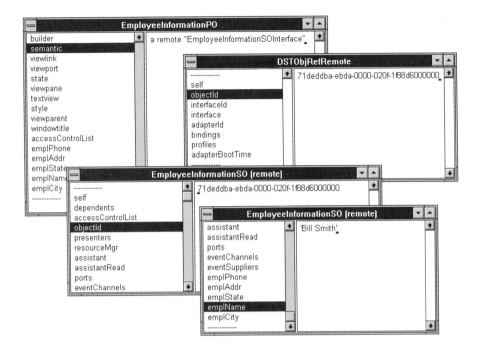

Figure 9–10. Smalltalk inspectors showing links between local presentation object and the remote semantic (data holding) object.

Figure 9–11 shows the code to create an Employee Compensation Object and place it under the *Employee Compensation Context* name space context. In the code, a containment link is created that creates a parent/child relationship between the newly created EmployeeCompensationSO and EmployeeInformationSO. The EmployeeCompensationSO is a container that will display a *view* of the EmployeeInformationSO. The *linkset* method returns an object that contains bi-directional link information for each object. The *title:* method updates the window title of the object.

There are many models for representing relationships between objects. There is a simple link model, where one object is aware of another's existence. There is a two-way link model, where each object is aware of the other's existence. The containment model has one object *containing* one or more other objects and is the *parent* object. There are different types of roles that objects may have in relation to one another. In an object-oriented system, an object of a certain class can also inherit behavior from a more abstract class. This also represents a relationship called a derived relationship.

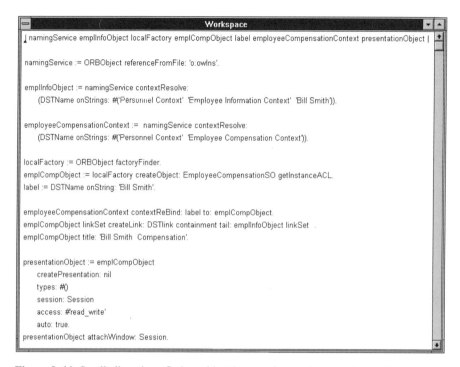

Figure 9–11. Smalltalk code to find an object in a naming context, create an object in another naming context, and create a containment link between the newly created object and the original object.

The last part of the code creates an entry under the Employee Compensation context that points to the Employee Compensation object and names it "Bill Smith."

Figure 9–12 shows the windows displayed as a result of the createPresentation method at the end of Figure 9–11. The *Bill Smith (on owl)* window is opened by double-clicking on the view window of the *Bill Smith Compensation* object.

Figure 9–13 shows the relationships between the naming contexts and the objects just created. The ORBObject contains the overall naming context. The naming context contains the Personnel context, the Personnel context contains two Employee contexts. The Employee Information context contains a link to the *Bill Smith* Employee Information object. The Employee Compensation context contains a link to the *Bill Smith* Employee Compensation context. The *Bill Smith* Employee Compensation object contains a parent/child link to the Bill Smith Employee Information object. This results in two ways of getting to the *Bill Smith* Employee Information object, either through the Employee Information context, or via the linked parent compensation object in the Employee Compensation context.

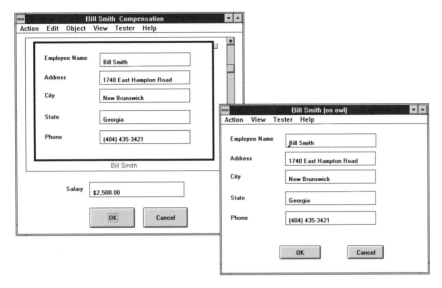

Figure 9–12. Windows created by the code in Figure 9–11. The compensation object has a containment link to the information object.

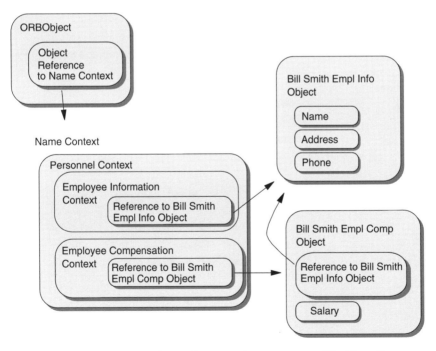

Figure 9–13. ORBObject contains a reference to the name context. The Name Context contains zero or more name contexts, any of which may have subcontexts. A context at any level may have a link to an object. The objects themselves, (such as the compensation object) may have a link to another object.

Figure 9–14 shows Smalltalk object inspectors opened on the relevant objects. The eleven o'clock position is the starting point. The inspect method on the ORB-Object naming service brings up the DSTNameContext object in the eleven o'clock position. Clicking on the bindings object, a Dictionary opens that contains all of the bindings for the naming contexts on this system. The *Personnel Context* is the first one. Inspecting the *Personnel Context* DSTNameContext brings up an inspector showing a structure like the overall naming context. The Personnel context contains two nested contexts. At this point, the inspector windows diverge. To the right of the bindings Dictionary are the inspectors that lead to the EmployeeInformationSO. To the bottom of the *bindings* Dictionary is the EmployeeCompensationSO. To the right of the EmployeeCompensationSO is the DSTLinkInfo object (created by the createLink: method) that points to the *Bill Smith* EmployeeInformationSO. The inspectors with the darker background are on a remote machine. The inspectors with the lighter background are on the local machine. This indicates that the local Employee Compensation object is linked to a remote Employee Information object. It can also be noted that the name service and various naming contexts are actually remote as well.

For informational purposes, we've used Smalltalk code examples and inspectors to view the links. In practice, visual tools may be used to build and maintain links between naming contexts, their contained objects, and links between the objects themselves.

Users may need to create and manipulate their own naming contexts for specialized purposes, such as creating ad hoc *databases* for personal use. For example, a personnel representative might decide to create a subcontext under Employee Information to track employees who are also members of professional organizations. She may want to create a naming context called *Professional Groups*, under which she creates several more naming contexts called *Rotary*, *Toastmasters*, etc. Under each of these, she may link the Employee Information objects for the employees in each group.

This is not to say that there are not other, perhaps better, ways to do similar things, such as by creating folders for each of the professional groups, etc. The power of using naming contexts is the ease of finding things. Containers, such as folders, by nature hold objects of different types. In a naming context, there may be rules for limiting the types of objects in the context to those of a particular type or class.

In the above example, all of the naming contexts are resident on a single-server machine when the objects are local or remote. Naming contexts themselves may have remote links to other naming contexts. For example, the naming context for Employee Compensation could be on a different machine from the parent Personnel Context. The Personnel Context would then have a remote object link to the Employee Compensation context rather than a local link.

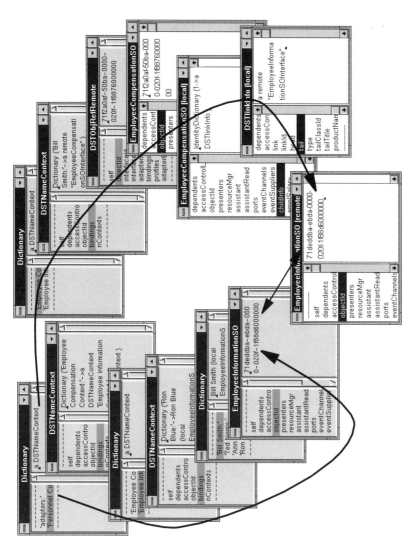

Figure 9–14. Smalltalk inspectors showing the links depicted in Figure 9–13. There are two paths to the information object, either through the Employee Information context, or through the Employee Compensation Context via the compensation object.

Once the objects have been created and linked to naming contexts, they may be found using the code in Figure 9–15. It shows that a DSTName string can be built from an OrderedCollection that contains all the names of the contexts that need to be navigated. The *emplCompObject* and *emplInfoObject* objects created in this code fragment would be able to receive a createPresentation message and open windows on their respective objects.

```
|emplInfoObject emplCompObject|

emplInfoObject := (ORBObject namingService) contextResolve:
        (DSTName onStrings: #('Personnel Context,
                        'Employee Information Context',
                        'Bill Smith')).

emplCompObject := (ORBObject namingService) contextResolve:
        (DSTName onStrings: #('Personnel Context,
                        'Employee Compensation Context',
                        'Bill Smith')).
```

Figure 9–15. Smalltalk code to directly access an object in either of the two naming contexts.

MAKING OBJECTS WORK TOGETHER (EVENTS)

Objects, like people, need to work cooperatively to perform useful work. Normal distributed object method invocations are generally enough to enable multiple objects to work together. The limitation in this form of interaction is that it generally must be synchronous. There are many occasions where asynchronous object communication needs to take place, which is where events come in.

In the CORBAservices model, there are three basic types of objects and two basic types of event communications. The three basic object types are supplier, consumer, and the optional event channel. The basic types of event communication are Push and Pull. That is, either the consumer pulls the event (via polling) or the supplier pushes the event (more of an interrupt-driven approach).

There are various and sundry uses for events. They can be used for real-time applications, like the annual report in Amy's session. They can also be used for interactions that take place over hours, weeks, or months. For example, a manufacturer may keep a running total of parts depletion. When a type of part is almost depleted, an event may be triggered that either informs someone that new parts are needed or interacts directly with the supplier to have more parts shipped in.

In Amy's session, the annual report object is a good example of a set of objects that use events in real time. The video wrapper object in this case is the supplier object. It is the originator of the events that the text and graphics object, the consumers, need to receive. The type of event model used by the objects will be the Push model. In this case, the video wrapper will send events to the consumers as the video progresses.

Since there is a one-to-many relationship between the supplier and consumers in this example, there will be an event channel. This event channel is simply an intermediate object that receives the event from the supplier and sends it to all the interested consumers. The relationship is depicted in Figure 9–16.

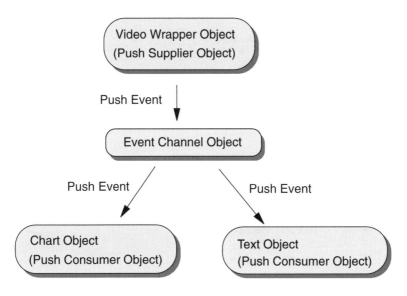

Figure 9–16. Video Wrapper Object supplies an event to an Event Channel object, which then forwards the event to two Consumer objects, the Chart Object, and the Text Object.

An event can be anything an object could be. It could be a simple message saying, in effect, *update yourself,* or it could be a complex object in its own right. In the annual report example, what is being passed is a simple message that indicates in which section of a commonly agreed upon outline the video object is. Figure 9–17 shows the relationships between the various objects in the annual report. Each of the objects in the annual report has a copy of the outline. The outline is a kind of map. All of the objects have relationships with the outline. The text object is supposed to show certain text at certain places in the outline. The chart object is supposed to show certain graphs at certain places. The video object is correlated with the outline as well. As the video progresses, the wrapper object, which is keeping track of which frame is currently being shown in the video, has related the frame numbers to locations in the outline.

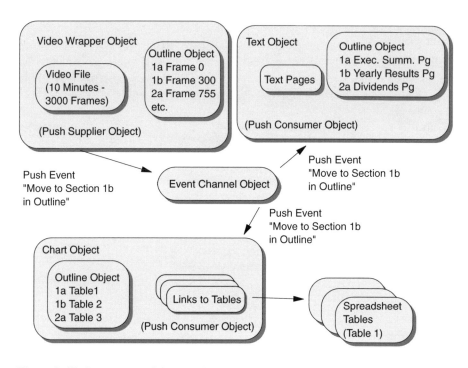

Figure 9–17. Components of the annual report object.

When a new section in the outline is reached, the wrapper object sends an event to the event channel. This event contains a string indicating the section now being presented in the video. The event channel forwards the event on to the two consumers. The value of this approach is that an additional consumer object, for example, a spreadsheet object, can be added to the report just by registering with the event channel. The new object only needs to understand the outline and how to connect to the event channel. It can then play its information back in unison with the other objects. One key to the relationship, of course, is the outline. It is simply a dictionary object that contains a set of strings linked to the events that need to take place. For example, for the chart object, the dictionary contains a relationship between the event and the particular table that needs to be displayed in the chart object. For the text object, the dictionary links the event string with the particular text object that needs to be displayed.

How does the technology work to support this scenario? We'll present a simplified version of the annual report. This *event mapper* application will show the basic event logic needed as a foundation for such an application discussed in the previous paragraph. In DST, the bundled sample chart object actually is a container object that can *contain* a spreadsheet table. If a table is dragged into the chart object, it displays the information presented as a chart — either pie, line, graph, etc. In the event mapper application, the chart object is linked to a wrapper object itself, which receives the event messages from the event channel and then drags the proper table object into the chart.

Figure 9–18 shows the event mapper controller and the text object and chart it controls. As the buttons in the event mapper are clicked, it causes the text object to advance pages and the chart object to change the displayed graph. This chart is displaying a graph that is the result of depicting the table it contains. Figure 9–19 shows what happens when the graph is double-clicked upon (opened). The embedded table is displayed with the spreadsheet cells visible.

The next series of figures show more of the internal relationships between suppliers, consumers, and the event channel.

Figure 9–20 shows the createEventChannel method. It creates a DSTEvent-Channel and initializes the supplier as a DSTPushSupplier. This sets up the channel as a vehicle for interrupts from the supplier to be passed on to the consumers. If the supplier had been set up as a DSTPullSupplier, a polling relationship would have been set up where the consumers would periodically ask the event channel if there were any events waiting to be delivered. This interrupt/polling design is not new, nor is the use of an intermediate process to handle such events. What is new is a standard, object-oriented distributed approach to the problem.

Once the event channel and supplier objects are created, a proxyConsumer object is created inside the event channel. This proxyConsumer will receive events from the supplier on behalf of the event channel. The statement "proxy-Consumer connectPushSupplier: supplier" associates the supplier to the proxy-Consumer from the proxyConsumer's perspective. The Smalltalk statement that follows connects the proxyConsumer object to the supplier from the supplier perspective. At this point, what is created is an event channel object, a supplier object, a proxyConsumer object inside the event channel object, and cross-links between the supplier object and proxyConsumer object. These relationships are shown in Figure 9–21.

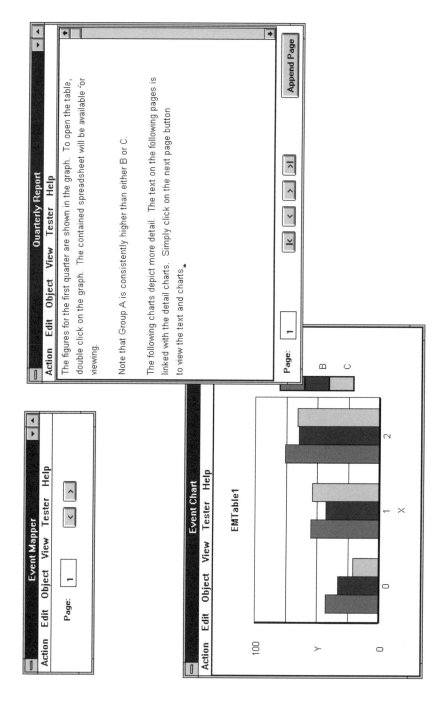

Figure 9–18. Event Mapper controller (supplier) object and text and chart (consumer) objects.

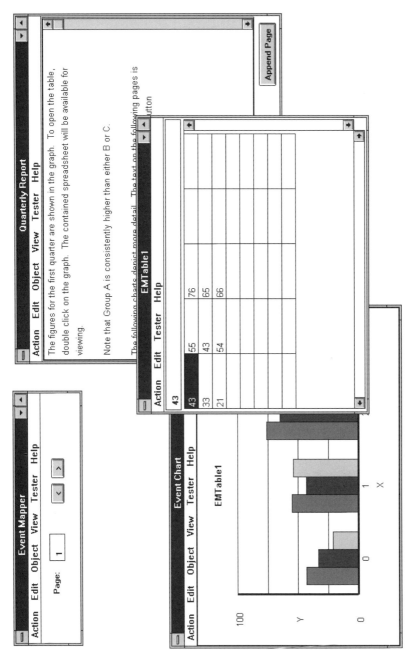

Figure 9–19. Table displayed when EventChart is *double-clicked*. EventChart is a container object that can display a view of the table object it contains.

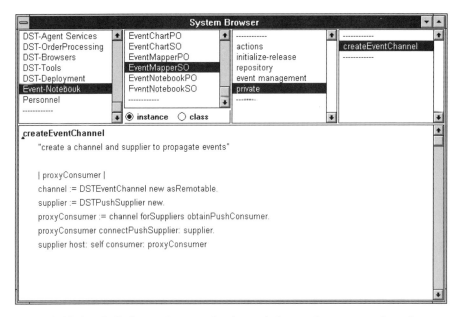

Figure 9–20. Smalltalk System Browser showing code for creating an event channel.

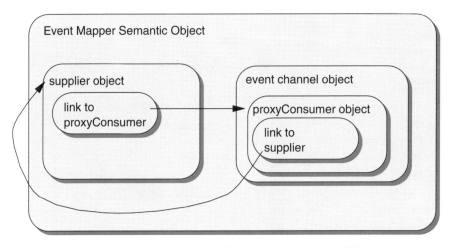

Figure 9–21. Relationship between event supplier and event consumer. When an event channel is involved, the supplier connects to a proxy object representing a consumer. If no event channel were involved, the supplier object would have a direct link to the consumer object.

Figure 9–22 shows the method inside the event mapper class that invokes the *createEventChannel* methods and then associates the *real* event consumer with the event channel. In this case, a consumer would be either the text object or the graph

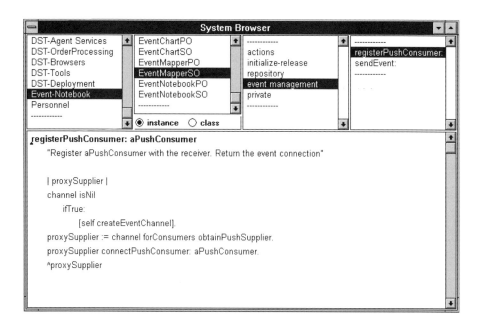

Figure 9–22. Smalltalk code to create a link from a consumer object to an event channel.

object. In this logic, once the event channel is created, a proxySupplier is created for the given consumer inside the event channel. The aPushConsumer reference is then connected to the proxySupplier, and the proxySupplier reference is passed back to the invoking pushConsumer to keep on hand. The relationships that now exist are depicted in Figure 9–23.

What the event channel gives us is a single object that has links to all the event suppliers and consumers. As more consumers (or suppliers) are added to the event channel, the other parties to the events don't need to know about them. As depicted in Figure 9–24, when the text object is added as an event consumer, only the event channel need know about it. Note that the proxySupplier objects are kept in a collection. This allows the event channel object to *broadcast* any events it receives to all of the relevant consumers simply by moving through the collection object.

Figure 9–25 shows the code used to send the event. The DSTEventChannel class provides a method called *processEvent*. The EventMapperSO class sends this event to its supplier object, which is of type DSTPushSupplier. DSTPushSupplier sends the event to its proxyConsumer in the event channel object. The code for processEvent:, inside the event channel's proxyConsumer object, is shown. It simply iterates through the collection of pushSuppliers (which are really proxy objects). The proxy objects pass the events on to their respective consumer objects.

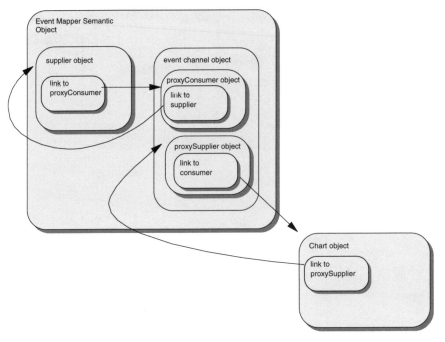

Figure 9–23. The relationships in Figure 9–21 with the addition of the consumer object. The event channel now has a proxy supplier object linked to the real consumer. The consumer object has a link back to the proxy supplier object. The event channel may have many proxy consumer and supplier objects.

KEEPING OBJECTS UPDATED PROPERLY (TRANSACTIONS AND CONCURRENCY)

In the information technology business, most of us have a good idea of what it means to do On-line Transaction Processing (OLTP), at least with a mainframe. Typically, that means that an IMS or SQL database stores information that is accessed via Customer Information Control System (CICS) or some other transaction control system. A transaction begins when we first read and update a record and ends when that record and any related follow-on records have been applied to the database and the transaction has been either committed or rolled back.

A transaction is defined as an information processing event that has ACID properties. ACID stands for Atomicity, Consistency, Isolation, and Durability. This means that a given transaction must be atomic, stand on its own, and be a *basic* unit of work — either it is all done or none of it is done. Consistency means that in the

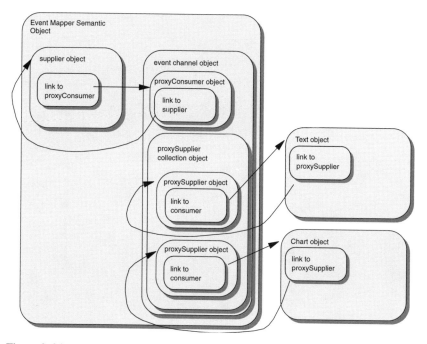

Figure 9–24. The text object has been added as another event consumer. The event channel protects the other objects from having to be aware of the addition of the text object.

same way that the databases and applications involved in the transaction were consistent (having integrity) before the transaction, they must be consistent after the transaction. Isolation means that the transaction stands on its own. It is neither dependent on other concurrently executing transactions, nor are the other transactions dependent on it. Durability means that the results of the transaction must be durable, having some level of persistence. The results must stick around — if there is no *result*, there was no transaction.

The introduction of client/server with the mainframe or a Unix or other machine as the server and a single workstation as a client complicates matters somewhat. The client in this case could act in a fashion similar to a dumb terminal, albeit with a more attractive look and feel. Once the client begins to actually get involved in the transaction, however, the complexity of managing the transaction, even a *traditional* third-generation-language-based transaction, goes up considerably. Of course, the significantly increased ease of use of the client over the terminal justifies the effort. Figure 9–26 shows the progression from a single-machine transactional environment to a client/multiple-server transactional environment. As is readily apparent, the complexity of the client/multiple-server environment is significantly greater than that of the single-mainframe environment.

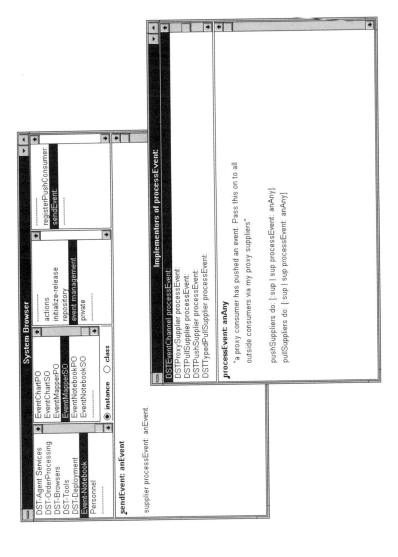

Figure 9-25. Smalltalk code used to supply an event and to process that event in the event channel. The event channel receives this event via its proxyConsumer object and then broadcasts the event to all of its proxySuppliers. The proxySuppliers then forward the event on to their respective *real* consumers.

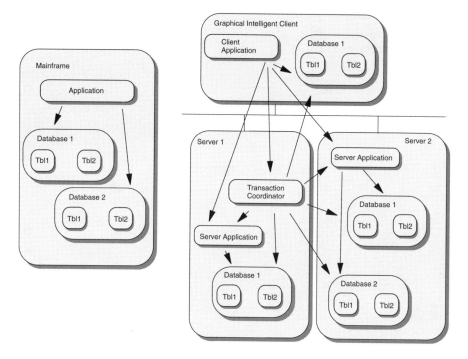

Figure 9–26. Single-system mainframe transaction processing is quite simple compared to the coordination required for multiple systems.

A great deal of work has been done in the area of distributed transaction processing and many, many successful implementations of distributed transaction processing have been in production for some time now. Standards also exist in this arena. X/Open and other groups have had published standards dealing with Distributed Transactions Processing (DTP) for several years. The X/Open Distributed TP Reference Model is a particularly good starting point (XOpen Co. Ltd, *X/Open Framework and Models*, Prentice Hall, 1995).

One of the key aspects of the DTP Reference Model is the two-phase commit or 2pc. The important objective of the 2pc is to provide the ability for servers to be able to maintain a state where a transaction can either be committed or rolled back if necessary. The 2pc allows cooperation to occur between the client and servers involved in the distributed transaction, with a failure in one server causing all servers to rollback their transactions. Figure 9–27 shows how a 2pc works.

The 2pc remains important in distributed object transaction processing. Distributed object transactional systems also need a cooperation mechanism and the 2pc provides that very well.

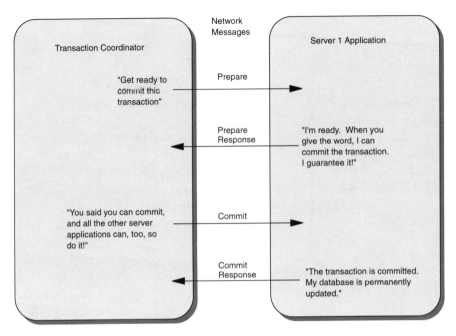

Figure 9–27. Two-phase commit. The prepare phase is followed by the commit phase.

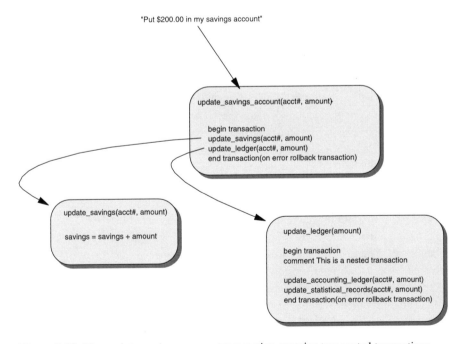

Figure 9–28. The *update_savings_account* transaction contains two nested transactions.

A second important aspect of DTP is the subtransaction, or nested transaction. A nested transaction occurs when a transaction is already in progress and another transaction begins in a nested fashion. Figure 9–28 shows a nested transaction. If the nested transaction is successful, all is well. If any of the nested transactions fail, the overall transaction fails.

Nested transactions are important with object systems as well. Nested transactions help to increase encapsulation, a goal of object-oriented systems. A component object may be a transactional object that contains other transactional objects. Since nested transactions are invisible to higher levels of a transaction (encapsulation), the higher-level transactional object is protected from changes in the code to the lower-level transactional objects.

A brief example will illustrate how DOT and DTP can be integrated. Assume we have two databases that need to be kept synchronized. These are a personnel database and an accounting database. When a person's salary is changed, both databases need to be updated. Figure 9–29 shows the *user-created* objects involved in the process. An employeeClientObject receives a method invocation to update its salary. Let's assume for the moment that the reference to the employeeClientObject is a semantic object that is connected to a window on a client workstation. This employeeClientObject, in order to update the salary of the employee, needs to update two different databases. One database is on the Personnel Server machine. This database is the Employee Database. The other database is the Payroll Database on the Accounting Server machine.

Since we don't want to have one salary figure shown on the Personnel machine and a different one stored on the Accounting machine, we need to use a 2pc protocol to make sure that either both servers are updated properly, or neither of them are. To facilitate this 2pc, we create *recoverable objects* on each machine. On the Personnel Server, we create an emplProfileRecObject. This is an object that can participate in a 2pc transaction. Similarly, on the Accounting Server, we create an emplPayrollRecObject, which also can participate in a 2pc transaction. Each of these recoverable objects will access their respective persistent objects in a database. If the 2pc transaction is successful, the salary figures in each of the persistent objects will be updated. If the overall transaction fails, when it is done, neither of the salary figures will have been updated. The transaction could fail because either one or both of the databases were unable to be updated for some reason.

Figure 9–30 walks us through the *housekeeping chores* that need to be done to make the 2pc commit happen. Step 1 is to create a Transactional Object, which we'll refer to as transObject. This object provides an easy-to-use interface to manage the transaction. Once the Transactional Object is created, we can refer to the *employee-ClientObject* as a Transactional Client because it is now able to invoke transactional operations, such as beginTransaction or commitTransaction, etc. Step 2 begins the transaction. When the transaction is begun, the transObject creates a Transaction

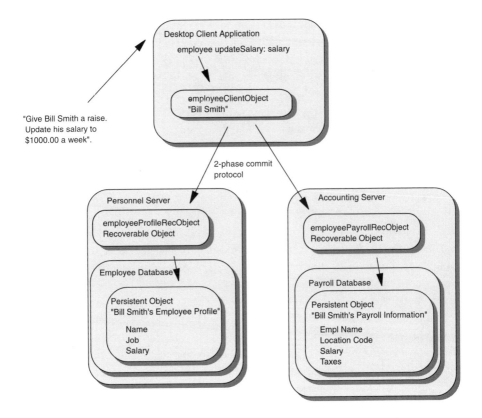

Figure 9–29. Employee and Payroll databases updated in a single 2pc transaction.

Object, which we'll refer to as *transaction*. This may be confusing. Why both a *Transactional Object* and a *Transaction* object? This will be explained a little later, after we introduce some other objects.

Step 3 is where we tell the transaction object that there are some other participants in the transaction. The resource objects are registered with the transaction object, which aggregates them in its internal *resource collection* object (that is, in its internal collection object that stores resources). Step 4 invokes the various method calls on the recoverable objects. These method calls perform the actual updating of the persistent stores of the objects, most likely databases. Persistence will be discussed in the next section, but suffice it to say, the recoverable objects will perform *begin work* and *create/update/insert/delete* operations in the method invocations activated by the messages sent by the transactional client. In this case, employeeClientObject sends one message to each of the recoverable objects, which perform *begin work* and *update* functions on the salary of Bill Smith.

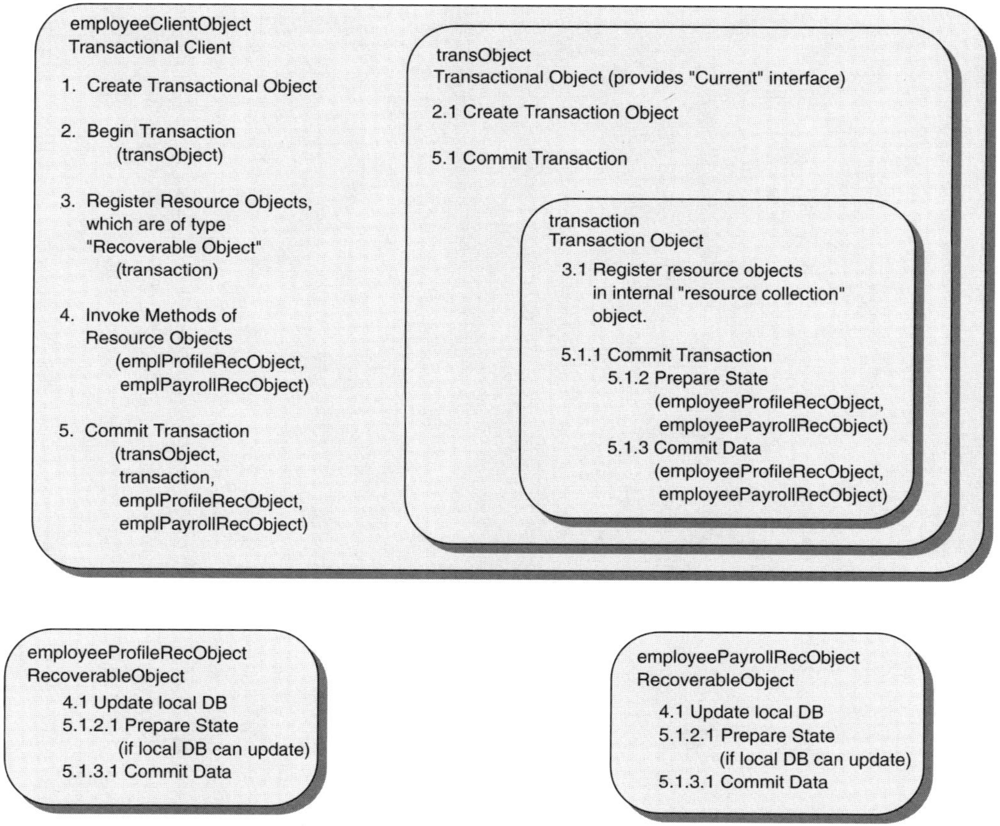

Figure 9–30. Objects and steps involved in creating a distributed object transaction.

Step 5 commits the transaction. The employeeClientObject sends a commitTransaction message to the transObject. It passes this message on to the transaction object. The transaction object message then sends *prepareState* messages to the two recoverable objects. Each of these recoverable objects then either updates their respective databases or else checks to see if an error occurred on an update that was performed earlier. If the updates were performed without error, the recoverable objects *vote* to commit the transaction. Next, at step 5.1.3, the transaction object tells the recoverable objects to *commitData*. The recoverable objects, upon receiving this message, perform *commit work* or its equivalent on their respective databases.

Once step 5 is completed, the databases are updated and consistent with one another.

Note that each of these objects is *distributable*. That is, they may be resident on different physical machines or in different processes on the same machine, etc. Any subtransactions may also be on different servers. This means that in a transaction and set of subtransactions affecting, for example, 10 different objects on 10 different machines, the coding is similar to that for transactions affecting 10 objects on one machine. This shows the inherent value of building facilities such as transactional services on top of distributed object frameworks. Since the location of the objects are *hidden*, including the actual machine/process they reside on, it is easier (relative to *traditional* development techniques) to make the objects part of a distributed transaction.

Figure 9–31 shows the code for the *updateSalary:* method for the transactional client object *employeeClientObject*. If you were satisfied with the explanation of the 2pc protocol above, you can skip this section. If you'd like to see more detail about how the various objects and interfaces fit together from a coding perspective, read on.

The first line of code creates the transactional object transObject. Next the transaction is started. The *beginTransaction* message sent to the transObject is what actually creates the Transaction object transaction as a component object of transObject. *beginTransaction* is part of the Current interface that is exported by the transactional object. The basic purpose of the current interface is to simplify coding. With *beginTransaction*, an implicit transaction context is created for the current process thread. The transactional object also provides simplified access to the coordinator and terminator objects, among others.

The coordinator and terminator objects are the ones that actually provide the resource registration, transaction commit/rollback semantics, etc. They have powerful interfaces themselves that are very flexible. As most of us have seen, flexible, powerful interfaces may also be difficult to initially use. The transactional object and the current interface are to hide some of that complexity from us. It is still there if needed.

In Figure 9–31, again, after the beginTransaction statement, the two recoverable objects are registered. In this example, the *create* message is sent to each of the recoverable objects and passes the employee object from the client to each of the

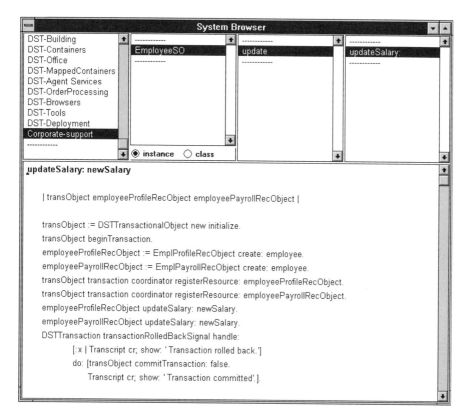

Figure 9–31. Smalltalk code for a transactional client object.

recoverable objects. They use this employee object to access the relevant persistent objects from their respective databases. Once the recoverable objects are created, they return their handles. Note that the recoverable objects may be remote, since we are using distributed objects. In the event they are remote, the object handles that are returned would actually be *DSTObjRefRemote* proxy objects.

The recoverable objects are then each registered with the transaction coordinator. The transaction is then committed. If the transaction is rolled back for some reason, a signal is raised that then allows the transactional client to perform any of its own error processing.

Figure 9–32 shows some of the logic in one of the recoverable objects. When the *updateSalary:* method is invoked, a *beginWork* is performed on the persistent store. The salary for Bill Smith is then updated, but the transaction is not committed. If the *updateEmp:* message returns an error, the returnStatus is set to an error condition, which will be used later.

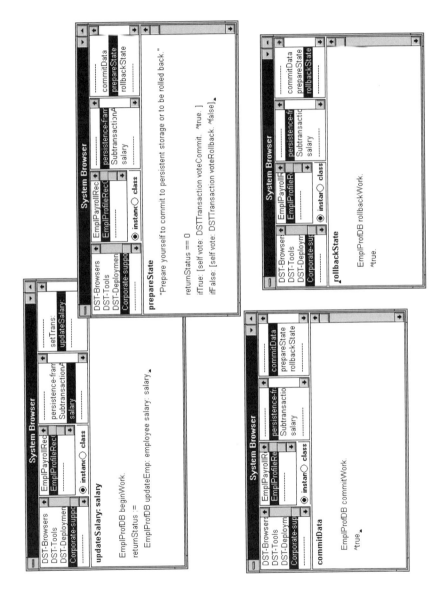

Figure 9–32. Smalltalk code for some key recoverable object methods.

When the transactional client sends the *commitTransaction:* message to the transactional object, the *prepareState* message is sent to the recoverable object. At this point, one of two things can happen. If the *returnStatus* from the previous database update is not an error, the recoverable object votes to commit the transaction. If that is the case, and all other participants in the transaction also vote to commit, then the recoverable object receives the *commitData* message. It then tells the database to *commitWork* on the database transaction currently in progress.

The other possibility is that either this recoverable object or another participant in the transaction voted to roll back the transaction. In this case, the transactional object will send the *rollbackState* message to the recoverable object. The recoverable object then tells its database to roll back the pending database transaction.

One of the benefits of a distributed object transaction service is that it can encapsulate object subtransactions. For example, in Figure 9–33, an enhancement has been made to the *employeePayrollRecObject* recoverable object. A need was discovered to

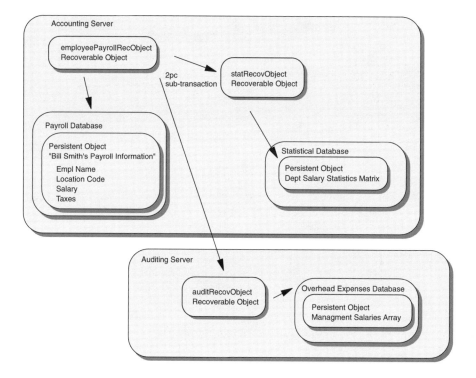

Figure 9–33. Recoverable objects may perform subtransactions without impacting the applications that use them.

have two other persistent stores updated with new salary information at the same time the Payroll database was updated. In this case, two new recoverable objects have been created. One is local to the Accounting Server, while another is on the Auditing Server, which is not co-located with the Accounting Server. This sub-transaction nested under the existing update transaction is controlled independently of the parent transaction.

Figure 9–34 shows the *updateSalary:* method in the employeePayrollRec-Object's class. First, updateSalary sends a *beginWork* to the database and performs its own update to persistent store. Then it creates a subTransaction under the existing transaction object. A reference to the *transaction* object was passed to the employeePayrollRecObject via the *setTrans:* method earlier. This is a distributed reference (*transaction* is a proxy object).

Figure 9–34. The *updateSalary:* method.

The updateSalary method then creates two recoverable objects. These objects are each registered with the subtransaction via the *registerResource* message. Note that they are registered with the subtransaction, not the *top* transaction. The next two lines send messages to the recoverable objects to have them update their respective persistent stores/databases. The subtransaction is then committed. The recoverable objects are then unregistered.

There is a great deal more power in a distributed object transaction service than we've discussed here. This simple example should give a sense of the kinds of work that can be done with such a tool.

STORING AND RETRIEVING OBJECTS (PERSISTENCE AND QUERY)

Storage of data is essential in any information system. Object systems typically refer to static or disk storage as *persistent storage.* It is referred to like this in order to indicate that the objects have retained their *objectness* but are simply placed in a location or on a medium that will support the object persisting outside of a process execution environment. In the chapter on object databases, we discussed persistence in the business context. In this section, we'll discuss the more technical aspects of persistent storage of objects.

Object databases (ODB) are the best persistent stores for objects. ODBs are effective at keeping objects in a state that is as similar to their run-time state as possible. There are many ways that ODBs store information. Some ODBs are actually relational database extensions. HP's Odapter, for example, is an object management engine on top of a relational database management system such as Oracle or Sybase. Other ODBs are effectively page fault mechanisms that access objects from disk via a method similar to an Operating System's (OS) use of virtual memory. ObjectStore database from Object Design is an example of this type of ODB. Still other ODBs support a form of three-tier computing where an OOClient, for example, a Smalltalk client, communicates over a network to an OOServer, also Smalltalk in the case of GemStone, for example, which is linked to a persistent store on the server.

There are other, non-ODB mechanisms for persistent storage of objects. Smalltalk, for example, has an image associated with the run-time process of a Smalltalk virtual machine. This image may be saved at the time of process deactivation and the objects within kept stored on disk until the process is re-activated. Smalltalk objects may also be *streamed* into a file for transfer to other images. This file is a form of persistent storage. Some people have indicated that fairly substantial projects may be implemented using only the Smalltalk streaming mechanism to handle persistent storage.

There are also class libraries that run in Smalltalk and C++ that support translation of language objects to the relational store. This is similar to Odapter (mentioned above) with the exception that objects need to be re-created with each access since the relational database itself has no notion of objects. This is changing, of course. There is a great deal of work in various standards bodies — OMG, ODMG, ANSI, and others — to develop standard object persistence and query standards. This area is in great flux, partly because there is already such a large investment in database technology, and partly because implementation solutions that take into account every type of database need are hard to come by. From a user's perspective, it isn't hard to get started, however. This section will be a bit of a departure from the rest of the sections in this chapter in that it will not discuss CORBA persistence services per se. Rather, we'll explore how Odapter, which translates from an OO environment to a relational one, provides for object persistence and query.

Odapter puts an object face on the front of relational databases. It supports the traditional mechanisms of relational databases with object orientation added in. With Odapter, a developer can create true objects that have state and functions. Odapter breaks objects down into three components: function, type, and object. An object is constrained by its type and accessed and controlled via its functions. A distinction is made between objects and types in a similar fashion to the distinction between object and class in Smalltalk. An object is an instantiation of a type but is separate from type. In fact, with Odapter, an object can be created as one type and then be converted to another type if necessary.

The architecture of Odapter is shown in Figure 9–35. Odapter can connect to either Smalltalk, C++, or JAVA applications, or with a line oriented or graphical browser. Since Odapter supports a client/server interface, with the application on one system and the database on another, it may be considered a basic distributed object system. There are many ways to architect an application to use an object database such as Odapter. Figure 9–36 shows an example where Visual-Works as a development environment could access the Odapter client, Distributed Smalltalk, or another object database client such as Gemstone's. On the server, the choices are either the *native* ODB server component or a DOT technology such as DST to access the ODB client as a process on the server. Also, using an ORB such as DST, the server side of the application can access relational mapping technologies such as ObjectLens or simply access the file system via object streaming.

Creating an object with an application or browser on the client will result in the object being created on the server. This object is then available to any other client application or browser accessing the same server. These objects are persistent and transactional. They may be large-grained, multiple-component objects or simple objects. For example, assume an object of type *person*. The class *person* has

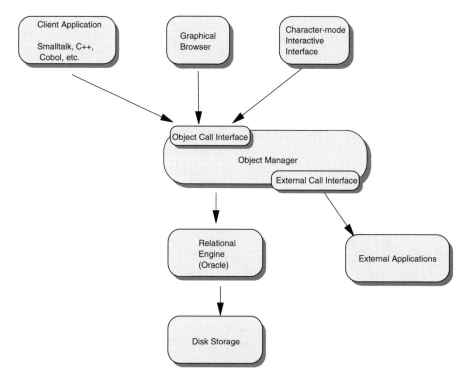

Figure 9–35. High-level view of Odapter architecture.

attributes name, address, and age. The following command will retrieve the ages of all of the persons in the database.

```
select name(p) for each person p where age(p) = 25;
```

The *person p* portion of the syntax defines the type to look for, while the *name(p)* syntax tells Odapter what object to return. This query will result in a group of *age* objects.

The use of *person p* saves the query writer from having to write

```
select name(person) where age (person) = 25;
```

The above example may not seem too difficult, but given that some queries are quite extensive and involve many object types, not just one, the shorthand provided by the *for each* clause is welcome indeed.

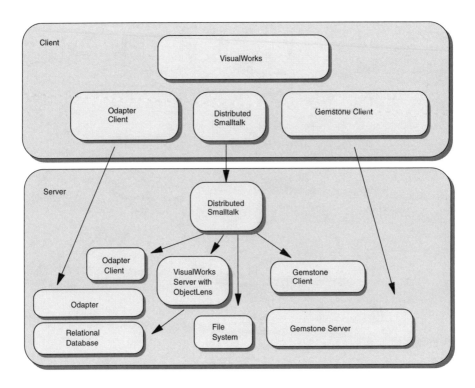

Figure 9–36. There are numerous ways to persistently store objects from a Smalltalk client. There are analogues to these mechanisms in the C++ environment as well.

Odapter is strongly typed, so any object to be inserted needs to be of a predefined type. Odapter supports several basic types, including all the atomic types (integer, character, etc.) as well as aggregate types like lists, bags, and sets. An Odapter database is formatted using a schema similar to a relational database. An object class *Person* for example, is created using this syntax:

```
create type Person functions (Name CHAR, Address CHAR,
                                    Age INTEGER);
```

Once an object is created in, for example, a Smalltalk application, it needs to be created in the database and then updated with the values in the Smalltalk application. To create a person object, this syntax is used:

```
create object as Person :persObject;
```

In this example, *:persObject* is the local variable that stores the object identifier of the person object that was created. At this point, the object identifier itself has a value (it is a *pointer* to a persistent store location), but there is no data in the object itself. The name, address, and age are *NULL*, or nonvalued.

To update the name and age of this person object, this syntax may be used:

```
update name(:persObject) := 'John Smith';
update age(:persObject) := 25;
```

Shorthand for the update is simply

```
name(:persObject) := 'John Smith';
age(:persObject: ) := 25;
```

To perform the create and update at once, this syntax works:

```
create Person functions(name, age) ('John Smith', 25);
```

From an implementation perspective, if the Person type is created with all of its atomic types at the same time, Odapter tries to put all of the types in a single table. If necessary, object pointers point from the base table to secondary tables. The case of an object having nonatomic types is handled like this:

```
create type Dept functions (DeptName CHAR, Manager Person,
                            Employees SETTYPE(Person));
```

Here, the type Dept has one atomic attribute and two nonatomic attributes. One of the nonatomic attributes is a single object, while the other is a group of objects.

The objective here is to show that object persistence doesn't have to be rocket science. There are many other fine object storage mechanisms, such as those supported by Object Store, GemStone, etc. Some of these object storage mechanisms provide a great deal of integration with C++ or Smalltalk, so that it is so easy to store objects, it becomes rather seamless. I chose the Odapter syntax because it is halfway between the *true* object databases and other object-relational adapters.

Make no mistake. There is a great deal of work involved in effectively and efficiently storing objects in a persistent fashion. The benefit of letting someone else write that code for you, either in a *pure* object fashion or in the form of a translator such as Odapter or VisualWorks' ObjectLens, etc., is that they have done the hard (and somewhat tedious) work of figuring out the mapping between object and relational storage formats, etc. In this case, it is better to let someone else do the hard work, while you simply work to make their implementation fit the needs of your applications.

Note also that much more power is available than discussed here. It is relatively straightforward to build very intricate *trees* of object relationships — either containment hierarchies (such as exploding parts for an airliner) or complex relationship graphs (many-to-many relationships in just about any information domain). The search capabilities are also very robust in the object storage engines we've discussed. It is possible in many of these engines to use CURSORs to manage large queries. Nested queries are also available in many of these tools.

Further, something available in object persistence mechanisms that is not so easily provided in more traditional storage mechanisms is transitive queries, where recursive functionality is available. For example, in the case of wanting a list of all of the parts used in an airliner, a query may be constructed to move down all the branches of a tree of parts, exploding out all of the parts, subparts, etc., to provide a complete, ordered list of components. Note that this can all be done in the database with no outside code being written. This would be the result of simply navigating through all of the relationships between parts and their component parts.

THE BROKER (ORB)

The Object Request Broker (ORB) "provides the mechanisms by which objects transparently make requests and receive responses. The ORB provides interoperability between applications on different machines in heterogeneous distributed environments and seamlessly interconnects multiple object systems" (*Object Management Architecture Guide*, Revision 1.0, Page Object Management Group Technical Committee Document 90.9.1).

In other words, an ORB establishes a path between a client and server object upon which message requests and replies can be made. Figure 9–37 depicts the basic communication path between a client object and a server object. The client machine sends the *open* message to the server object. If the object is local, it would simply receive the message and open itself up.

If the object is remote, however, there is actually a proxy object on the local machine that represents the remote object. The proxy object contains reference information that *points* to the real object on another machine. This reference information is the server hostname, the server adapter ID, and the unique object reference for that object on the server. The proxy object receives the *open* message and passes it on to the remote machine. On the remote machine, the object request broker has a *read* waiting on a well-known port, expecting incoming requests. When the request to access a

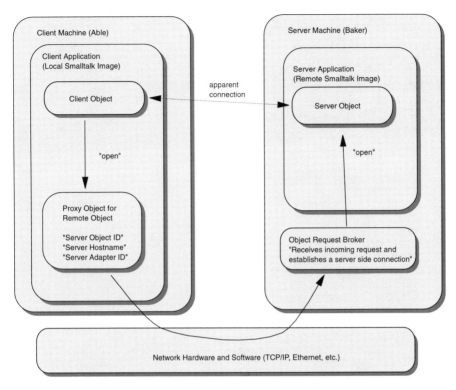

Figure 9–37. Apparent and true connections between a Client Object and a Server object.

server object is received, the ORB takes the message and passes it on to the client object. Once the communication channel is opened, the client and server object can continue to interact without the need for the ORB. More about this later.

In order to do this in real situations, the ORB must also take into account that the hardware and software on the client and server systems may not come from the same vendors. This need for interoperability has driven the CORBA 2.0 standard.

For additional clarity, Figure 9–38 shows the Distributed Smalltalk implementation of the object request broker. This code is certainly not for the faint of heart, but it's not really all that complicated. If you simply believe that it works, bypass the next few paragraphs. If you just have to understand how the real guts of an ORB work, read on:

Line 1 is the method signature or *entry point name*. Lines 4/6 document the starting of the ORB in the system log. Line 7 sets up a connection queue, allowing for a backlog of 20 connection requests. Line 8 sets up error handling for the connections. Line 9 permits multithreading of connections. Line 10 is a variable that

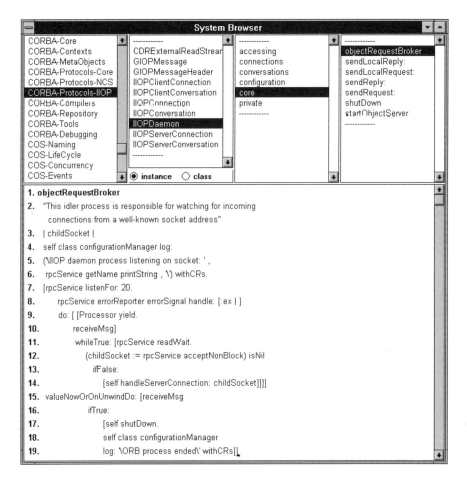

Figure 9–38. An object Request Broker.

is set to True before the objectRequestBroker method is started. Line 11 is where the ORB actually waits for an incoming request. If a request comes in, line 12 executes, and the network (via rpcService) returns a childSocket. The childSocket is a connection link.

If the childSocket is isNil, control returns to the rpcService readWait command in line 10. The acceptNonBlock message simply doesn't *block* or wait on the read. In line 14, the ORB is telling itself to hand the connection over to the server process handling the connection on behalf of the client object.

Lines 15 to 18 are the shutdown code. It is activated when an exception is sent to the ORB telling it to close down. Because this is Smalltalk, these last lines are actually *activated* first, but just wait around until the exception, while allowing the code in the receiving block (lines 7 to 14) to execute first.

Interestingly, while it is a rather involved exercise to interpret the code in this ORB, the objectRequestBroker method listed above is really not doing that much. All the ORB is doing is *answering the phone* and handing it to the client. On the other hand, this really is the essential point. The ORB is simply acting as a *broker*, passing requests for communication back and forth between clients and servers. Note that it is not handling all of the communications traffic between the client and the server. It is only handling the initial connection. After the connection is established, the client and server can communicate as much as they wish without needing help from the ORB. The ORB, then, is *establishing the connection*. After that, its job is finished.

While the simple ORB method shown above is just the beginning, the concepts and technology that are built upon it is becoming more *robust* all the time. At the foundation of the ORB is the concept of link abstraction. That is, if you abstract and encapsulate link information, protecting the software developer or end user from needing to know about it, you provide a great deal of power and flexibility to the user and developer.

Built on the ORB are techniques and software that allow objects to tell where they are located and helps them get connected to other objects. These services are similar to those discussed in Chapter 2 that are used by object languages on a single system. The important differentiator here is that the objects, whether large or small, can be located on a system nearby or far away.

On a single system, one object is linked to another via a pointer. This pointer is usually a memory pointer, or 16- to 32-bit address. An object reference between objects on different systems, or between objects on the same system in different memory/process spaces must contain additional information. This distributed object reference must contain information on the process to access, the system to access, and the object to access within that context. There are a number of methods to accomplish this, but in the CORBA 2.0/Interoperability specification a standard method is outlined. It is called the *General Inter-ORB Protocol* and is more specifically defined on top of the TCP/IP network protocol as the Internet Inter-ORB Protocol (IIOP). In the IIOP the information that needs to be known for a client object to access a server object is the *host* or server machine internet address (15.31.136.164, for example), the TCP/IP port number that the *target agent* or server ORB is listening on, and the *object_key*, or reference to the specific object accessed via that ORB on that machine. These three pieces of information get the request to the correct server, the correct process on that server, and the correct object in that process.

As an illustration of this interoperation, let's use a DST example. Assume machine Able is a desktop client. It is displaying a window showing various icons

(Figure 9–39). One of the icons points to an object called *Bill Smith*. It is an employee information object. Clicking on this object opens it and shows a window with information about Bill Smith. The object that contains the actual information about Bill Smith is on the server, machine Baker.

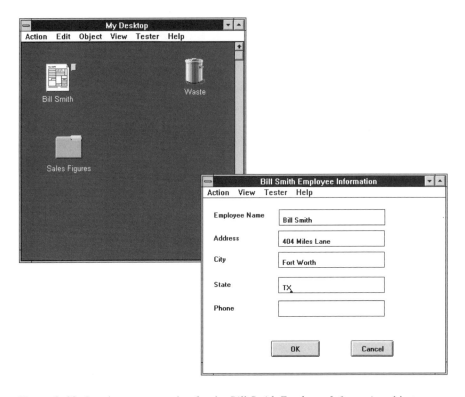

Figure 9–39. Opening a presentation for the *Bill Smith Employee Information* object.

When a user on the client machine (Able) wants to access the *Employee Information* object for Bill Smith, she double-clicks on the proper icon on her desktop. Then what happens in the system to get the information for her?

When she double-clicks on the icon, the local application (desktop container object) activates and sends a message to the local proxy object. The local application neither knows nor cares that the real object is on a remote system. The *proxy* object on the local system, placed there as a placeholder for the true object, receives the request for information and sends the message to a *client conversation* object (Figure 9–40). This client conversation object marshals the parameters and creates a client connection object. This client connection object

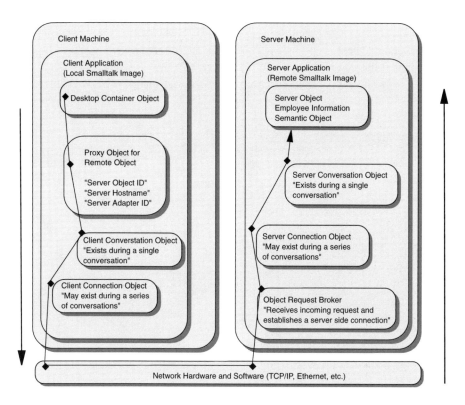

Figure 9–40. There are various *support* objects involved in communication between a client and a server object.

maintains the actual network link for the client side of the conversation. While the client conversation object only lasts for the length of one message *conversation*, the connection object will last as long as necessary, perhaps until the ORB is shut down.

The client connection object passes the message to Baker. The ORB on Baker receives the message and creates a local *server connection* object. The server connection object maintains the socket connection on the server side. It also persists through multiple-message conversations.

The server connection object creates a server conversation object. The server conversation object activates the local server object, unmarshals the remote message and its parameters, and invokes the proper method with the message and parameters. The server object opens as it is supposed to. At this point, since the object needs a window to show its data, it also opens a remote object. This time, the Employee Information Semantic Object is the *client* and an *Employee Information Presentation Object* on Able is the *server*. This is shown in Figure 9–41. The important fact here is that at any time, one object may be a client, while at another time, the same object may be a server. In similar fashion, while a desktop *client* may at one time have a client object that is requesting services of another object, at another time the desktop machine may be providing *server* functionality to an object residing on a server machine.

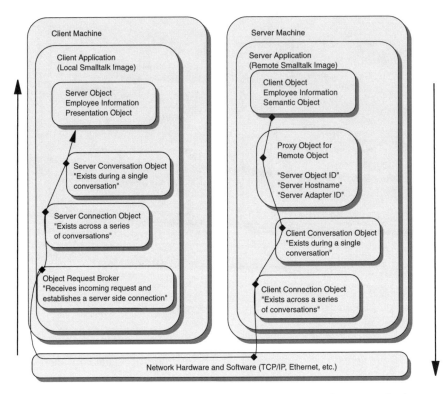

Figure 9–41. A presentation object (normally considered a *client object*) may also become a server object. In like fashion, a semantic object may become a *client object*. Being a client or server depends on which side sends the transaction and which side receives and processes the message.

THE CONTRACT: INTERFACE DEFINITION LANGUAGE

Any time that two parties reach an agreement, there is a contract that documents the agreement. This contract may be nothing more than a handshake, or it may be several volumes thick. The contract lays out the terms of the agreement and is meant to be fully understood by both parties. In a sense, a contract is what is needed between a client and a server in order for them to be able to work together. The contract provides boundaries for the interaction of the client and the server but also provides freedom of action within those boundaries.

OMG distributed object contracts are written in Interface Definition Language (IDL). IDL is a standard language that defines the interfaces that a client or server object will support. These interfaces consist of the types of objects or variables that the client or server object will accept, as well as the method or function signatures that the client or server object supports.

The IDL for an interface may be a single simple method call, or a large set of methods that interrelate. As an example, Figure 9–42 shows some of the IDL for the employee information semantic object. Specifically, the *setEmplInfoAddrStateCityPhoneBy* message is shown. This message is called by an employee information presentation object. It updates the key information in the employee information semantic object. The method also updates any other open employee information presentation objects, as shown in Figure 9–43

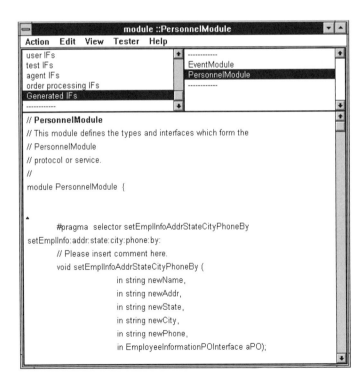

Figure 9–42. Interface Definition Language.

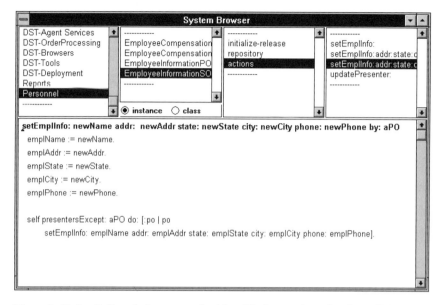

Figure 9–43. Smalltalk code for a semantic object. The loop at the end updates all the presentation objects that it may have other than the one that originally sent the update message.

Interface definitions, like object instances, need to be tracked. The way this is handled with distributed objects is with an Interface Repository (IR). An IR is a persistent storage mechanism where interface definitions are stored and read from. The IR is kind of a dictionary for interfaces. Also, since objects can inherit functionality from parent objects, interface definitions must be able to inherit from parent interface definitions. This is supported in a CORBA-standard IR.

An important aspect of being able to use a contract such as an interface definition is to have it available for use. When a server or client object publishes its interface, it is useful to be able to look at it easily. This is accomplished via a browser. A browser is able to look at the IR and present the information it holds in an easy-to-use manner. In DST, there is a graphical IR browser as shown in Figure 9–44. This browser allows a user to navigate through interfaces and walk down any inheritance trees. It also provides a textual view of the information in the repository, as was seen previously in Figure 9–42.

If a software developer needs to access certain server objects, he or she can determine what interfaces the object supports by using the IR browser. It will provide such information as the parent interfaces, the types of objects the server object accepts, and the kinds of methods it supports. Note that IDL is necessary but not sufficient as a method of fully determining the use of an object interface. Good documentation on the functionality of the methods exported by the object is still necessary. It is incumbent

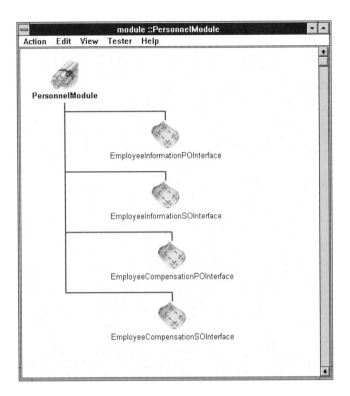

Figure 9–44. Graphical interface repository browser.

on the server object designer to not only express the interface in IDL for ease of translation to client implementations on other platforms but also to document the behavior of the server methods. This can be done via comments in the IDL. In the case of DST, these comments would be available to the viewer via the IR browser.

Other information can be supplied in browsers. It is useful to server object developers to know what clients have *subscribed* to the interfaces exported by their server objects. It is also useful to know what different server objects are accessed by any given client object. There is opportunity for additional add-on utilities to the IR browser that would keep track of providers of server objects, subscribers to the objects, etc.

While it is necessary to have the IR document the interfaces available on a server, it is also necessary for the server objects to know what interfaces they are represented by in the IR. Figure 9–45 shows two methods that link a server object (class) to the IR. The CORBAName method used by distributed objects in DST returns the name of the CORBA interface for the class. *abstractClassId* returns the universal unique identifier for the class. This UUID will be valid for this class of object for whatever server the class has objects on.

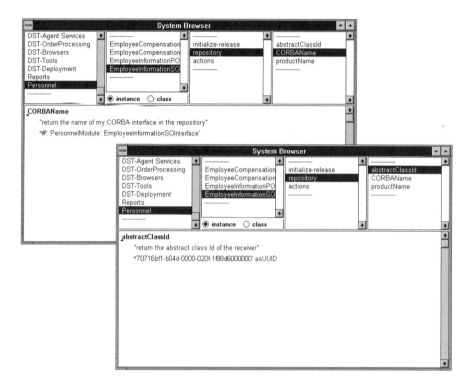

Figure 9–45. System-generated methods that link a server class to the interface repository.

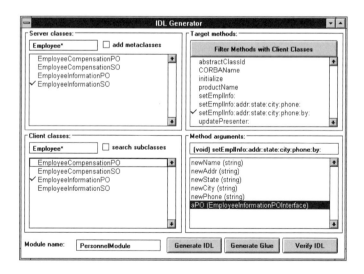

Figure 9–46. Tool to system-generate IDL for a class.

Figure 9–46 shows DST's IDL Generator. This tool provides an easy-to-use interface to automatically generate IDL for a class. It is an example of the kinds of tools that can be developed to make DOT easier to manage.

This chapter has discussed DOT as it has been applied using CORBA standards and Distributed Smalltalk. This application of DOT illustrates some of the flexibility and power available to developers of DOT applications. While it remains a significant undertaking to develop distributed, client/server applications even with CORBA technology, the tools are improving, bringing development of CORBA-based enterprise applications within reach of most developers.

10

FROM DESKTOP TO NETWORK: OBJECT LINKING AND EMBEDDING

OLE has become a de facto industry standard for integration of desktop objects as well as for integration of server data sources. OLE was invented by Microsoft and is supported on the various flavors of Microsoft Windows (3.1, NT, 95). OLE is also supported on various other platforms and by some CORBA-based software providers (such as Orbix from IONA, and ORBPlus from HP).

OLE has various components, as shown in Figure 10–1. As can be seen in the figure, OLE is based on another Microsoft-developed standard, the Component Object Model or COM. COM is the underlying framework that supports OLE. According to Microsoft:

> The Component Object Model is an object-based programming model designed to promote software interoperability; that is, to allow two or more applications or *components* to easily cooperate with one another, even if they were written by different vendors at different times, in different programming languages, or if they are running on different machines running different operating systems. (*The Component Object Model Specification*, Version 0.9, October 24, 1995)

OLE/COM shares common objectives with OMG CORBA. Where OMG is attempting to foster cooperation between systems suppliers, software vendors, and users, Microsoft is viewing the problem from the perspective of desktop users and from the perspective of Independent Software Vendors (ISVs). *How can a word*

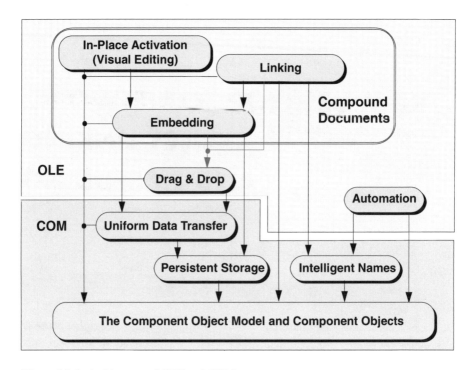

Figure 10–1. Architecture of OLE and COM.
Source: Microsoft, The Component Object Model Specification.

processor access the best sorting algorithms available? What is the best way to make desktop components interoperate? How can server data be most effectively accessed from a client?

From a strict, technical perspective, OLE/COM lacks some of the refinement of OMG CORBA. For example, OLE lacks robust event, transaction, concurrency, and relationship services. OLE does have advantages in the *linking and embedding* aspects of graphical application integration. The greatest advantage of OLE/COM, however, lies in the fact that it is implemented on so many computers already that it is a very appealing vehicle for ISVs to extend the capabilities of their products. Indeed, various CORBA-based software providers are already offering links from OLE/COM to their tools. These bridges will allow companies to implement integrated OLE/COM — CORBA-based networks without needing to do the integration of the two models themselves. One of these integrators will be discussed in this chapter.

Also in this chapter, we will discuss Next Computer Inc.'s Portable Distributed Objects layer network that enables OLE automation over a network. We will also discuss Microsoft's own remote automation for OLE. All of the examples will be done using Visual Basic. Although C++ is a much more powerful language than Visual Basic, it is also much more difficult to understand how things work using C++. Visual Basic, like Smalltalk, lends itself well in explaining how distributed object technology, as expressed via OLE, works.

Object purists will object that Visual Basic is not an object-oriented language, and rightly so. VB 4.0 does contain the *class* construct, however, and has allowed for the creation of *objects* containing both function and data (in the form of procedures and properties) before VB 4.0. It would be correct to say that VB is currently *object based*, and on its way to becoming object-oriented. Indeed, some industry pundits assert that VB, with its easy-to-use interface and many add-on components, will present a simple challenge to Smalltalk as the *easy-to-use* object-oriented language.

LINKING AND EMBEDDING

The two primary aspects of OLE are the compound document architecture and the automation facility. These are distinct capabilities that may or may not be integrated in a given application. As of this writing, compound documents are not network enabled directly but may take advantage of other network facilities to appear network enabled. The compound document architecture is important in that it is the beginning of what is needed to fully enable the kind of environment discussed in Chapter 1.

Any user of Microsoft Word or other such tools may be familiar with how to create compound documents. A Word user clicks on the Insert menu and then on the *object* selection item. This results in a dialog box, as shown in Figure 10–2.

Selecting a media clip, for example, brings up the media viewer application. The user can then open a video file from within the media viewer and update the Microsoft Word document with the video clip (Figure 10–3). In the case of the media viewer OLE object, the first frame of the clip is actually *displayed* in the Word document, while the linked OLE object also holds the file name of the original video file. In Figure 10–3, the file containing the video clip actually resides on a file server. The file name of the remote file is contained in the OLE object in the word processing document. This is useful for video objects since it is rather unwieldy to carry a 50-megabyte video file around embedded in your otherwise 50-kilobyte word processing document. It points out a weakness in the media viewer's implementation of OLE, however, in that it relies on the file system to maintain links. If the video file is moved or renamed, the link is lost. It is up to the user of the document to update the location.

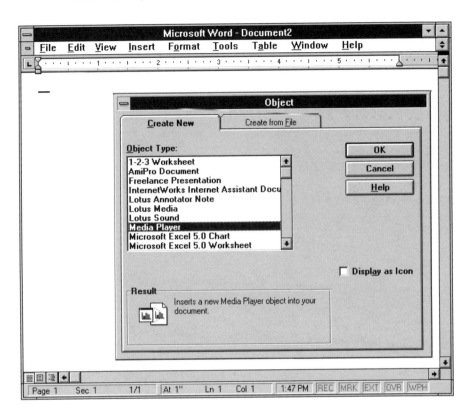

Figure 10–2. Inserting an object in Microsoft Word.

One way this problem can be overcome is with OLE *embedding*, where the source document is fully contained in the container document, so it's not possible to lose a connection to it. The problem with embedding, of course, is that updates aren't easily performed. Also, if the embedded document is very large (like the AVI file), the size of the container document is rather unmanageable. Another possibility is to use *monikers*, which encapsulate a type of name, as well as the functions that permit an application using that name to access the object that the name refers to. The moniker, then, encapsulates the access method for accessing a particular object.

While building distributed applications using *network* versions of OLE's linking and embedding functionality is appealing, this functionality is still relatively immature. The network implementation of OLE Automation is better defined. The remainder of this chapter will limit itself to the network implementation of OLE automation as expressed via remote automation.

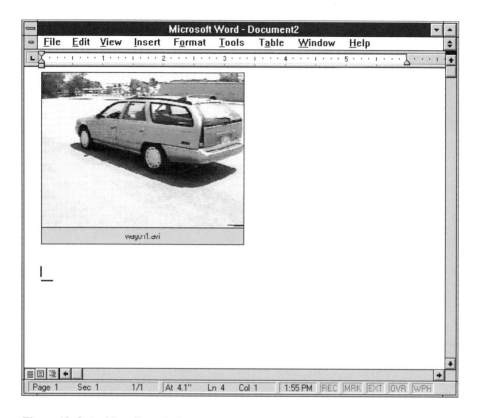

Figure 10–3. A video clip embedded in a Microsoft Word document.

OLE AUTOMATION

OLE automation was developed as a way to give an application *remote control* over another application. A Microsoft Excel macro could use OLE automation to access a database via Microsoft Access. A Microsoft Word macro could access and control Microsoft Project projects and tasks, etc. This type of control could extend over just about any other type of application. An application that enables telephony applications could export an OLE automation interface that could be used by other applications. A specialized database application could export an OLE automation interface. This list goes on.

OLE automation distinguishes between OLE clients and OLE servers. An OLE server exports an interface that contains methods and properties. The methods are actions that the server will perform on behalf of the OLE client. OLE server properties are characteristics of an object. These characteristics are publicly accessible data from the OLE server object. The data may be stored in the object or may be retrieved by the server object from another source (i.e., flat file or database).

A Visual Basic application becomes an OLE Automation server when one or more of its class modules' Public property is set to True, thereby exposing that class to external use, and the application is configured as on an OLE server. Once the server has exported an interface, other work needs to be done to make that interface available over the network. We'll use a simple example, drawn from the calendar object of Amy's work session in Chapter 1 to illustrate how OLE client and server technology works. Then we'll get into discussion of how network versions of OLE work.

OBJECT CREATION

To create an OLE automation object from a client in Visual Basic, the CreateObject function is used. Figure 10–4 shows the relationship between a simple OLE client and server. The OLE Server Proxy is a mechanism provided by OLE to handle out-of-process servers. The OLE Client starts the server, tells it to do work, then stops the server. This, of course, is the most basic lifecycle. There are many other possibilities, such as creating pools of OLE servers that run continuously and respond to requests, etc.

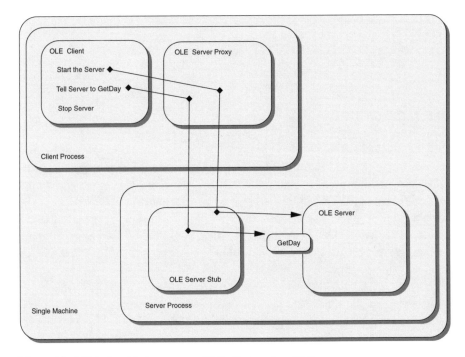

Figure 10–4. Relationship between an OLE client and an OLE server.

Figure 10–5 shows the VB form and code for a simple OLE client. The form presents day-at-a-glance calendar with tabs for each day of the week. When the form is loaded, the client application connects to the server application. When a given day of the week is requested, the local *datebox_update* method is invoked. This method invokes the *GetDay* method in the server. Closing the form sets the local object to *Nothing*, which releases the connection to the server. Figure 10–6 shows the *GetDay* function method in the CALServer OLE Server. It uses the information passed from the client to access the appropriate appointments from the server database.

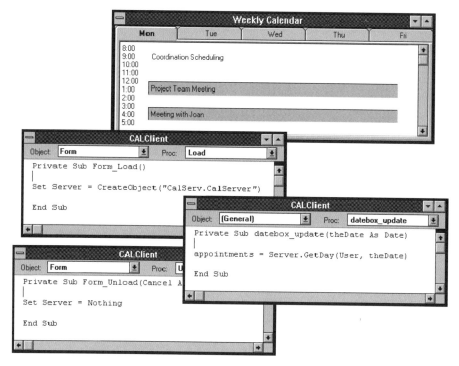

Figure 10–5. Visual Basic code for an OLE Client.

Note that there is no extra effort required to *marshal* parameters between the OLE client and server. Visual Basic handles this translation for the developer.

FINDING THE SERVER

OLE uses the Windows system registry to store object interface information. Figure 10–7 shows the available references and object browser in VB. The References dialog lists available server references on the client system. The Object Browser allows more detailed browsing of OLE server interfaces. For example, the GetDay method of the *Calendar OLE Server* is shown. At the bottom of the dialog, the GetDay method is documented as a function that returns a variant type parameter.

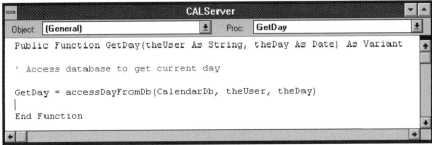

Figure 10–6. GetDay OLE server function.

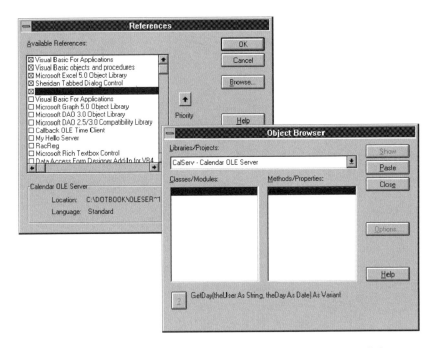

Figure 10–7. Visual Basic OLE Control References and Object Browser dialogs.

Figure 10–8 shows the *Remote Automation Connection Manager.* This tool is used to show both available local interfaces as well as allow a user to redirect the invocation of an OLE server to another machine. In Figure 10–8, CalServ.CALServer is highlighted. It is shown as being registered locally. The information displayed here is from the system registry. Figure 10–9 shows the Connection Manager again. In this example, the CalServ.CALServer has been set to remote (upper-right-hand portion of the dialog) and the server machine has been set to *deptsrv.hp.com*, with *TCP/IP* as the network protocol to be used. With this configuration, a local CALClient process will be routed to *deptsrv.hp.com* when it performs a *CreateObject* on *CalServ.CALServer*, even if a local server is available.

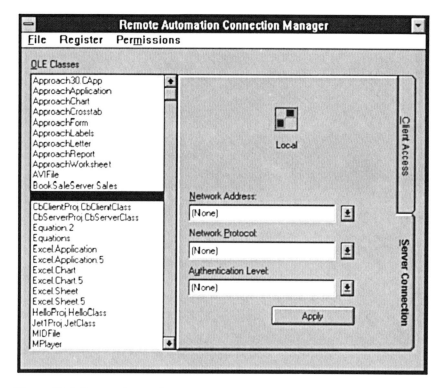

Figure 10–8. Remote Automation Connection Manager application included with Visual Basic 4.0 enterprise edition.

DISTRIBUTION

When the local workstation runs the OLE client in Figure 10–5, OLE will see from the system registry that the server needs to be invoked from a remote machine. Figure 10–10 shows the message flow when the server is remote. The

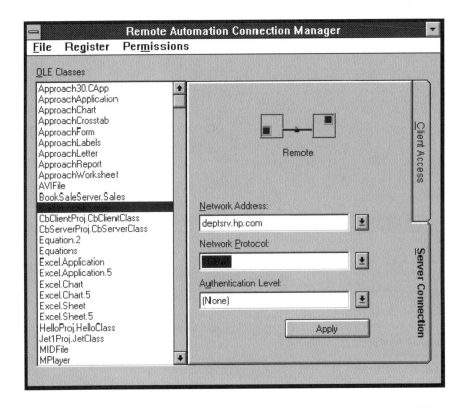

Figure 10–9. CALServer object will now be accessed from *deptsrv.hp.com* server machine.

client object tells OLE to start the server. (1) OLE checks the system registry to see if the server is local or remote. (2) Because the server has been set to remote by the Connection Manager, OLE uses the local remote automation (RA) object. (We'll discuss the remote automation object in a moment.) When the client tells the server to *GetDay*, (3) the RA object passes the message on to the remote machine. (4) On the remote machine, the RA stub passes the message on to the OLE proxy. (5) The OLE proxy passes it to the OLE stub in the server process. (6) The OLE stub passes the message to the actual OLE Server. (7) The response from the server follows this chain back.

On the remote machine, a process called the *Automation Manager* is launched to receive incoming RA requests. The Automation Manager then starts the CALServer on the remote machine if it is not already active.

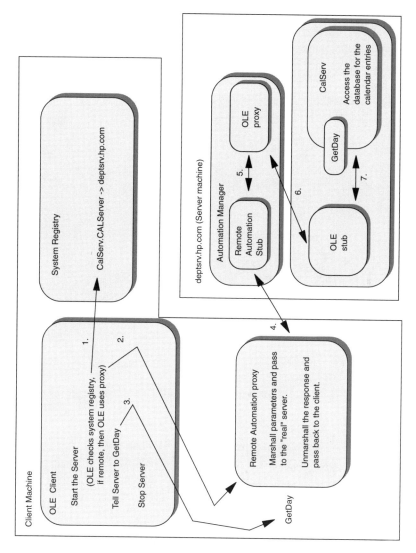

Figure 10–10. OLE client/server message flow for a remote OLE server.

The RA object here is similar to the kind described in Chapter 9. It is a local object that acts on behalf of the remote server object. Its primary functions are to maintain the connection with the remote object and to marshal and unmarshal the parameters between the client object and the network. The Connection Manager makes it easy to change an OLE Server from local to remote and back again. Since the system registry can also be updated by a VB program, the connection can be altered programmatically as well.

NeXT Computer has done some enhancement of OLE automation on their own. They have extended OLE to communicate via their own Portable Distributed Objects (PDO) architecture (Figure 10–11). Since PDO is inherently distributed, it allows for distributed OLE (D'OLE) as well.

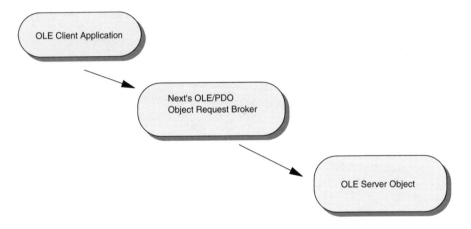

Figure 10–11. NeXT's PDO can connect an OLE Client and OLE Server via its own ORB.

Figure 10–12 shows an application that uses PDO and D'OLE. The application creates a server *ORB* object using *Nextorb.OLE*. This is the PDO object request broker. It then creates a server object by sending the proper message to Nextorb. Nextorb then passes the message to the OLE server object. As you can see in Figure 10–12, the *connectTo* method of Nextorb allows the client to specify a given hostname (remote machine name). With this architecture, D'OLE enables a client application to access the same kind of OLE server object on multiple remote hosts or the local host. D'OLE will also allow the integration of other PDO servers, such as UNIX or Nextstep servers, with OLE applications.

OLE remote automation and PDO can also be used to either directly run or front end standard Windows applications. This allows the Windows applications,

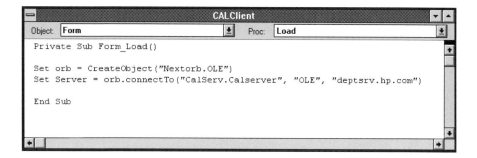

Figure 10–12. Visual Basic code to use the OLE interface for NeXT's PDO ORB.

such as Microsoft Excel, to function as a component of a client/server application. Figure 10–13, for example, shows using either PDO or RA to access Excel remotely. Figure 10–14 shows the VB code used to run Excel remotely. Any OLE automation function can be sent over the network, directly accessing the remote application. This allows for the creation of *Excel servers*, for example. While it is certainly possible to simply share files between Excel clients, the value of servers is that macros can be built, server databases can be transparently accessed, and the Excel server can be viewed as a *compute server*, where a powerful PC server can be allocated for use as the compute engine without requiring processing power on the client.

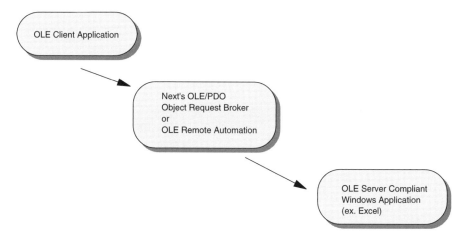

Figure 10–13. An OLE client can use PDO or OLE remote automation to launch and control a copy of Excel or other Windows application on a remote server.

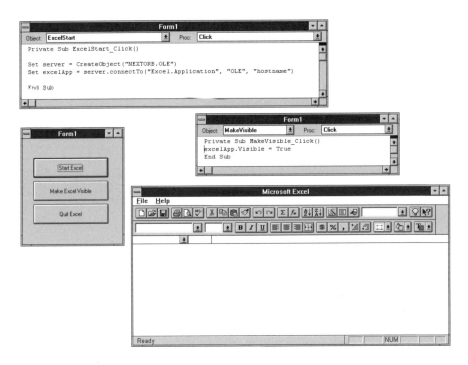

Figure 10–14. Visual Basic code used to start and remotely control an Excel spreadsheet application.

Figure 10–15 shows a sample of the functions available for a remote application from an application such as Microsoft Excel. Nearly any activity that a user might perform with Excel can be automated with OLE automation and then made usable over a network with remote automation.

SERVER INTEGRATION

Various types of software are being produced that can integrate OLE with other types of distributed object technology. Iona Technologies, for example, has integrated OLE with its Orbix software. This technology uses a software gateway approach to integrate CORBA and OLE. Figure 10–16 shows the architecture of the ORBIX/OLE integration. The OLE client application sends a message to the OLE server embedded in the Orbix integration code. The OLE server passes the message to the Orbix client, which then sends it to the actual server, which may be on a different machine.

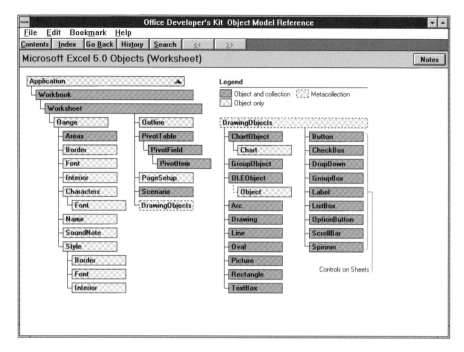

Figure 10–15. Microsoft Excel exports much of its functionality via OLE. These functions can be accessed remotely via remote automation. *Source: Microsoft Office Development Kit.*

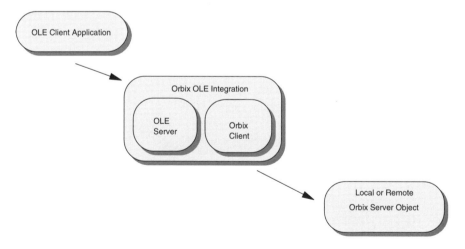

Figure 10–16. Iona's Orbix can translate OLE remote automation messages to CORBA messages.

While using Orbix is a bit more complicated than VB remote automation, it provides significantly more flexibility. There is the capability to create smart proxies, for example, which can locally cache object data. Orbix allows the user to access sophisticated object location mechanisms. It also brings interoperability with a CORBA 2.0 compliant server application and platform.

EVENTS

Visual Basic allows for the passing of an object reference from a client to a server. With VB Remote Automation, the client can create a local object and pass its reference to the remote object server. When the remote server needs to inform the local client application of an event, it can use the previously passed object reference to pass a message. This permits the creation of such applications as event services where the server interrupts the client. The client can always use a polling procedure as well, of course, where the client periodically invokes a method in the server to determine any changes in server state that may be interesting to the client.

It would be possible to create the kind of robust event services in Visual Basic with remote automation that is present today in such environments as Distributed Smalltalk. Various third-party vendors are at work doing just this sort of thing.

SERVER THREADING

CORBA implementations such as DST provide for threading of server connections. That is, when a connection from a client to a server is made, a process thread is spawned to manage the connection. This type of activity is not automatically performed in remote automation, so it needs to be managed by the software developer. There are means to do this, and sample applications bundled with VB show how it may be accomplished.

CONCLUSION

Remote automation as expressed via Visual Basic is a good start on the road toward DOT for OLE. There are many other capabilities of OLE that have not been discussed here, but the reader has an idea of what OLE can begin to do when it is extended over a network. OLE will be a major component in distributed applications of the future because of three factors: (1) It is a solid foundation for Microsoft's continuing investment. (2) Powerful third-party enhancement products will continue to be created for it. (3) CORBA suppliers will continue to create gateway products to tie it into OMG's architecture, guaranteeing it a place at the enterprise solutions table.

11

THE WEB

The World Wide Web (WWW), via various standards bodies such as the WWW Consortium and the Internet Engineering Task Force, is another point of gravity for DOT evolution and deployment. Hypertext Transfer Protocol (HTTP), Hypertext Markup Language (HTML), Common Gateway Interface (CGI), and other evolving technologies such as Java, due to their simplicity and ubiquity, are powerful forces in shaping the future of distributed objects. Figure 11–1 shows a client browser, which sends messages to httpd (HTTP Daemon, or background server process), which either accesses files directly, or uses CGI to run a program to access the application/data it needs.

At first blush, it might appear that current Web technologies are not good candidates as DOT software. HTML is certainly not a *pure* OO language. There is no inheritance, no polymorphism, no true abstraction. It is primarily a document description language. From an OO perspective, HTTP isn't much better. It does use a Uniform Resource Locator (URL) that contains something that looks like a method name, a remote machine identifier, and a machine-specific item identifier. This *scheme://machine.domain/full-path-of-file* syntax contains all the information needed to remotely access a server *object*, but it is limited. CGI does a good job of invoking the right server program and passing information to it. This can be viewed as a form of server object invocation, but performance is a concern, since CGI doesn't even do a remote procedure call, let alone a true remote object invocation. CGI actually invokes an entire program (albeit perhaps a small one) to perform the *method* assigned to it by the client.

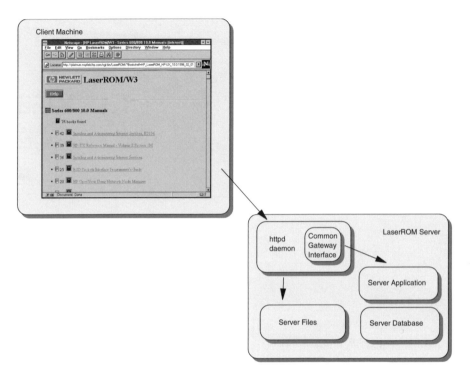

Figure 11–1. A Web page can connect a user to server files or to a CGI application.

If one takes a less dogmatic view of distributed object technology, how the
Web fits in becomes more clear. A fundamental benefit of object technology is
encapsulation. That is, you don't have to worry about the format of some data
because an object interface is provided for you that hides the actual implementation.
You also don't have to worry about *where* something is (in memory or on a network)
because the object interface (and related services) also protects you from needing to
know that information as well. The Web, at its most basic, provides encapsulation
of network data and processes. The user is presented with a document that has
hyperlinks to other documents. These hyperlinks, coded in HTML (with included
URLs), provide pathways to access more detailed or related information without the
user needing to know where the data is, how it is formatted in storage, or what
access method will be used to get the data.

While the Web mechanisms in most prevalent use — HTML, HTTP, and CGI —
are very limited, they do indeed provide both data and function encapsulation as well
as location encapsulation. These characteristics permit these technologies to be catego-
rized as distributed object technology.

Because the Web thrives on diversity (and because there is such a sore need for help for the basic technologies that make up the Web), there are many other object-oriented and object-based technologies coming to the fore. These are various and sundry, from efforts by individuals and universities to efforts by major standards bodies and influential corporations. *Java ™, Microsoft's™ ActiveX™, Netscape Frames™* and *Plug-ins™*, and many other technologies are efforts by various groups to improve Web client browsing capabilities and server data access. Some of these will be examined here for their possible impact on the Web as distributed object technology.

NAMING ON THE WEB

Naming in the Web community is somewhat less structured than it is in either CORBA or OLE. As compared to using naming contexts in CORBA, which are oriented to enterprise domains, or system registries in Microsoft NT or 95, which are machine oriented, the Web uses the Uniform Resource Locator (URL) mechanism to find objects. The URL mechanism is a very simple, straightforward approach to network object access. If there is an HTML document on machine Able called /$wwwroot/DocumentB.html (Figure 11–2), the URL for that document is

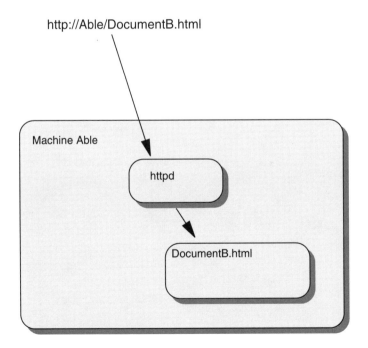

Figure 11–2. Universal resource locator is used by an httpd daemon to access a file from a server.

http://Able/DocumentB.html ($wwwroot in this instance refers to the root WWW document directory of the given machine). This name is distributed object based in the sense that it encapsulates the machine name, file location, and type of access (http, ftp, gopher, etc.) in one name, the URL.

There are pros and cons to this from a DOT perspective. On the pro side, the method is simple and easy to implement. On the con side, if an object migrates, the pointers to that object may become out of date. For example, assume you have a URL *http://spock/filea.html* (that I like), and I therefore provide a link to on my document, which has the URL *http://kirk/filex.html* (Figure 11–3). Then along comes another user who needs the information on //kirk/filex.html and creates a link to that page from his own. Later, you decide to move your document elsewhere, to mccoy from spock (Figure 11–4). The URL on my page is no longer good, and other users who have been accustomed to coming to your page via mine can't do that either.

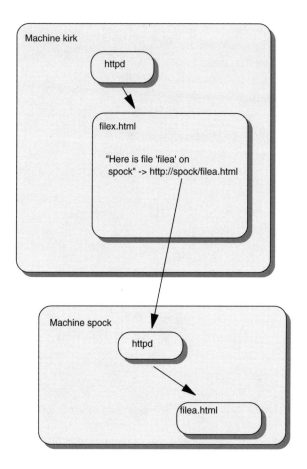

Figure 11–3. HTML document containing a link to another HTML document.

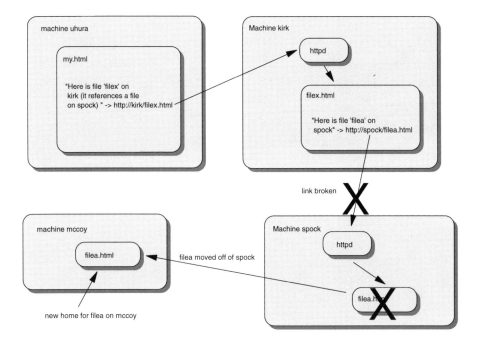

Figure 11–4. Web links can not be updated when a document is moved. The formerly linked document is then no longer accessible.

Some browsers have the capability of "noticing" that a URL has changed and automatically follow the forwarding address. While this is helpful, it is only a patch on the problem. There are other proposals under consideration that will address this problem better.

RELATIONSHIPS

Several techniques are evolving to establish more complex relationships between HTML documents. The most prevalent means today of showing relationships are with *textual* or visual URL hyperlinks from one HTML document to others. Other mechanisms have been developed and are becoming more prevalent. Frames allow subdividing an HTML document into several subdocuments in a Web browser window. These frames are then individually accessible and may have their own links to different network *objects* (Figure 11–5). Use of frames would allow a user to create his or her own *front page* with links to different news sources. Numerous possibilities exist with the use of frames. They can give an executive a composite view of the status of his subordinate departments' Web pages (which may

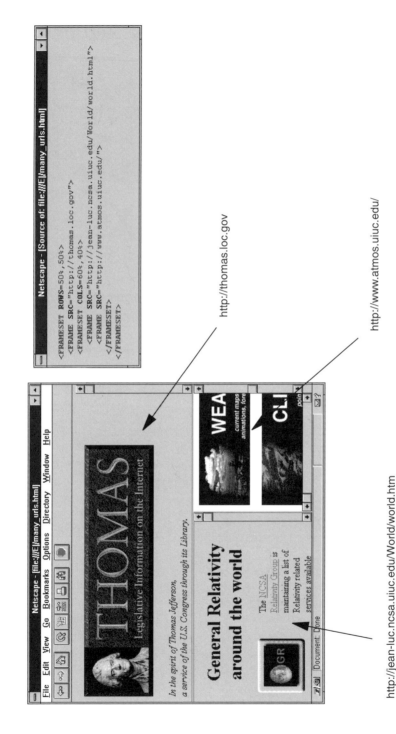

```
Netscape - [Source of: file:///E|/many_urls.html]

<FRAMESET ROWS=50%,50%>
<FRAME SRC="http://thomas.loc.gov">
<FRAMESET COLS=60%,40%>
<FRAME SRC="http://jean-luc.ncsa.uiuc.edu/World/world.html">
<FRAME SRC="http://www.atmos.uiuc.edu/">
</FRAMESET>
</FRAMESET>
```

http://thomas.loc.gov

http://www.atmos.uiuc.edu/

http://jean-luc.ncsa.uiuc.edu/World/world.htm

Figure 11–5. Use of frames can make a Web page a compound document, with *view* links to other Web pages.

be updated daily or hourly). They can provide a financial analyst a composite view of stock and other financial information from numerous internal and external sources, and so on.

Plug-ins are another component that can be embedded in an HTML document. Plug-ins can do anything from enable embedded video applications to access of remote objects. Plug-ins have access to URL callbacks. This means that a developer could create a plug-in that will, for example, allow a user to enter some query information (or update information) and then transmit that information via a URL. In this sense, a plug-in is a component object with the HTML document being the container for it. Note that since a URL is not limited to HTTP, the transmitted information may be in SMTP format, telnet, or ftp format (or any other format that may be defined and in general use).

REMOTE OBJECT INVOCATION

Remote object invocation is a problem that is typically solved by use of proxy objects. That is, when a local application needs to invoke an object method on a server (to access data, for example), the local application will generally access a proxy object. This proxy object encapsulates location and identification information about the true object and passes the message invocation on accordingly. Another interesting solution to the problem of remote object invocation involves bringing the object to the client machine to execute.

This solution is both possible *and* viable. Various technologies do this, such as some object databases (which *fault* when an object is found not to be in local memory and the object is *swapped in*). Java does this. Most of the current implementations of Java are primarily used to "jazz up" a screen by providing some form of animation. In this role, Java is really simply a portability solution. It allows someone to build an applet that will run on any of the various platforms that are supported by a Java-compliant browser.

Java, and like technologies, may also be shown to be *proxy-replacement* technologies in the sense that, if you want to invoke an object method on a remote machine, you simply download that object (with its respective data and function) and run it on the local machine.

For example, assume you are running Netscape and are using a banking application. This banking application has an *account object.* In this account object is stored your name, address, balance, last month's transaction summary, etc. A proxy object solution would provide a local proxy object that points to the actual account object on the remote server. A Java applet can be written, however, that encapsulates all the interfaces required to interact with the account object. When you access this account object from the banking application (via Netscape), the account object is actually downloaded to your client (methods, data, and all) so that you can access it and update it locally. When you have finished and say "I'm done!", the applet can transmit the altered account object back to whence it came. This is depicted in Figure 11–6.

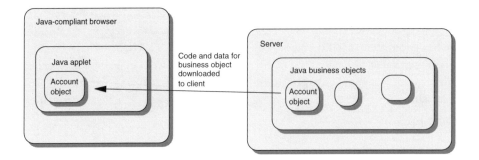

Figure 11–6. Business objects implemented in Java. Both the data and the function of the object can be downloaded to the client for use.

There are strengths and weaknesses to this approach. A large object can take a while to download. On the other hand, it may be *cheaper* to download a large object if there will be lots of interactions (method calls) on the object. In this sense, downloading is a form of caching. The value of Java technologies is that your client application didn't have to be written to know about every single type of object access you will ever perform. As long as it understands Java, it won't stand in the way of you and your object. Proxy objects, on the other hand, presume that there is code in the local client application that interfaces between the actual user and the proxy object itself. With Java-type technologies, the user interface can come with the object.

SERVER OBJECT INVOCATION

The HTTP daemon (httpd) process on the remote server has two primary methods of accessing server data today. One is via the file system. If a file system is in the file space that the daemon has access to, it can be accessed and displayed on the client browser. Another method is to use the Common Gateway Interface (CGI). CGI basically allows the daemon to run a program and pass various parameters to it. This is not a particularly elegant solution from a distributed application perspective, but it works.

The CGI program invoked by the httpd daemon is free to either pass a file back to the daemon for transmission back to the client or the program itself can send http responses to the client.

There are various and sundry methods being devised to bolster this currently rather weak server-side application structure. Netscape, Spyglass, and others, for example, have defined additional APIs on their versions of the httpd daemon that use more refined means of function access, such as procedure calling mechanisms, etc. Other software providers are creating versions of httpd daemon that have built-in gateways to their own very sophisticated software technologies. Oracle, for example, has developed a daemon that can invoke Oracle database stored procedures directly. ParcPlace-Digitalk has developed a daemon in its VisualWave Server product that can directly invoke Smalltalk methods that can dynamically build HTML screens and do other complex tasks.

Additional standards are likely to be developed in the Web server arena. It is a fertile area and is likely to use ideas developed in other settings such as CORBA and OLE. Understanding these other, more sophisticated server object technologies will yield insight into how the Web will evolve.

Part IV

Integrating DOT into Today's World

It is always good to look closely at where you have come from when looking at where you are going. In Part IV, we discuss how distributed object technology builds on the shoulders of what is present today. In this closing section, we discuss how DOT builds on legacy systems, leverages CASE, and impacts the organization.

12

LEVERAGING LEGACY SYSTEMS

Much of today's mission critical data is still resident in mainframe databases. Most of today's business logic is hidden away in 10-, 20-, or 30-year-old COBOL applications. These resources are too valuable to simply throw away and rewrite from scratch. Even the most effective implementation technology (such as distributed object technology) is often better used to enhance existing systems, rather than just replacing them entirely. This chapter will discuss ways to use DOT to supplement, rather than simply replace, existing legacy systems.

WHAT IS A LEGACY SYSTEM

A legacy system is any system currently in production. This includes both ancient assembler programs as well as brand new C++ ones. To be a legacy system is not bad — this appears to be implied by the name. A legacy system is one which has been left to us. More important than the technology that a piece of software was written in is the *way* it was written. Does the software have modular interfaces? Does it have good documentation? Are the different subsystems well defined? Are the interfaces between the application and system services such as operating systems and databases localized in well-defined parts of the application? Is the code portable? Does it use open interfaces wherever possible? Given these guidelines, an old COBOL program may be more useful from a leverage standpoint than a brand new Visual Basic program.

Each of these questions leads to other questions and to answers that give an idea of how leverageable a legacy system is toward future development. Most legacy systems were written with some thought toward the future. The key is, how well did the designers *see* what was coming. Also, many legacy systems were written so long ago that it was impossible for them to imagine today's environment. Many legacy systems have been well maintained but were written, for example, as batch master file updates using tape at a time when processor and memory costs and limitations were the most important factors in systems design. This means that the structure is hard to adapt to today's needs.

An encouraging fact is that DOT is one of the best technologies to come along for the encapsulation of legacy systems. It combines two of the most advanced means of reusing and enhancing legacy software and hardware. Object technology is very good at helping to leverage small or large components of software systems. Distributed systems or client/server technology performs well at leveraging existing hardware by accessing the hardware using another machine via the network. In combination, distributed technology and object technology provide very flexible means to encapsulate most legacy systems.

Assume, for example, a legacy terminal-based system to perform lookup and update transactions on a database. It was implemented using COBOL and IMS databases on a mainframe. The software was not written with desktop clients in mind. The business rules are embedded in the logic of the programs. Database calls, business logic, and terminal interaction functions are intermingled in each module. There is good modularity between functions, but certain database segments are accessed by different modules in different ways. So, we have a mixed bag here — good modularity from a function standpoint, but poor modularity from a data standpoint and a technology standpoint. Also, since the existing system is an on-line system, there is reuse in the interactive sense. That is, a batch, host-oriented system is more difficult to leverage into a client/server distributed system than is an on-line system.

Multiple options exist for leveraging this legacy system. The most favorable involves encapsulating categories of terminal transactions as objects. Each terminal transaction becomes a function or method call for the given object. These are not objects in the truest sense, since there is not a complete encapsulation of the data in a given object. Since certain data in the databases is accessed by multiple functions, there is the possibility that some of the data could be updated by different *objects* in the *new* system. While this is not ideal, it may be structured into a manageable problem. Another aspect to this solution is that the objects are fairly *large-grained.* This is not as optimal a solution as a new system written in a language that can export fine-grained objects, such as Smalltalk or C++, but the result can still be very leverageable.

The resulting system is depicted in Figure 12–1. To any client on the network, the legacy system appears to have an object interface. To access the application, the client creates a local object proxy and sends messages to that proxy, just as to a pure object server. The middle-tier server translates the object invocation into function calls against the server. The middle tier server may cache certain information locally in either a transient or permanent fashion to improve the performance of the client transactions. As other new systems are built, they can leverage the power of the object interface on the middle tier. The middle tier can also become the focus of continued modernization of the legacy system, hiding the changes from the clients accessing the system.

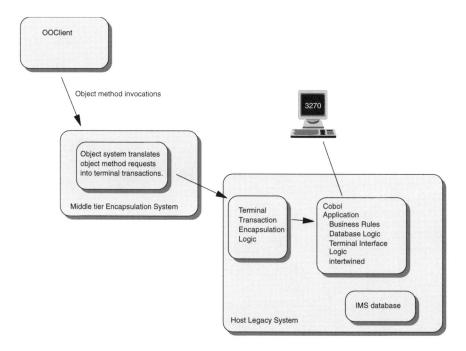

Figure 12.1. Encapsulating a legacy system with a middle tier.

Alternately, the legacy system can be maintained as is indefinitely, if business needs do not change. As new applications are built, they can gradually take over the interfaces that are currently exported by the existing legacy system and its object interface.

13

CASE FOR DOT

There are those in the computer industry today who will say that "Computer Assisted Software Engineering (CASE) has failed" or that "CASE is dead." This may be true depending on the definition of CASE that is used. CASE, in the abstract, is the use of modeling at the application analysis and design phase and the use of persistent repositories for doing impact analysis, etc., even the generation of code from models. It is not dead. In this sense, CASE is very much alive and well.

On the other hand, CASE meaning structured analysis and design activities, which generate models that are depicted in data flow diagrams and entity relationship diagrams, etc., is passing from the scene. As discussed in Chapter 3 on object modeling, the use of the object paradigm to describe business information is much richer than traditional structured methods. Object modeling itself, however, benefits from the use of computer-based tools just as much, if not more, than structured CASE did.

This is not to say that CASE for object modeling is sufficient, as structured CASE proponents used to argue. There is still great need for *lower-case* tools such as prototyping tools, code browsers, etc., as there ever was. High-level modeling of business systems using object-oriented CASE tools along with *brass-tacks* tools such as GUI-generators/prototypers, code browsers/object inspectors, etc, is sufficient to meet the need.

In the distributed applications arena, it is even more important to do effective modeling of business information to effectively capture and reflect business objects and events in information systems. Distributed systems are inherently more complex than traditional mainframe systems, even as they are more flexible.

In the distributed systems world, there are indications that simulation of the application is nearly as important as modeling the business objects and their interaction. Indeed, the future may hold that traditional structure CASE may become a simulation of distributed object systems using sophisticated CASE-like technology. As a system evolves, software analysts may view real-time simulations or summarizations of how objects on the network are being used. These simulations may be integrated with business changes to create new business and technology objects that can then be seamlessly integrated into the distributed object network in real time. As users continue in their work, they can become aware of these new business objects and their constituent services. Using on-line help and tutorials as they perform their work, the users can smoothly integrate these new software capabilities into their workflow.

MODELING DOT APPLICATIONS

Object modeling is becoming more refined. In this time frame, the second-generation case tools are becoming more pervasive, as consolidation moves through the object modeling ranks. How to model DOT, however? The major benefit of modeling is to help the software and business analyst look at the overall picture and refine it iteratively, without the expense of actually implementing a system, and then having to go through the laborious processes of refining the system, as the users better understand how the system can aid them in performing their tasks.

One answer lies in rapid prototyping. As users define their needs, the software analyst can begin to create a client GUI application that has no true back end and refine this prototype in the presence of the user. Simultaneously, the same users or other users can be working with server modelers to create the business objects that will support the client application as well as other applications to come. These business objects can be *painted* using a graphical modeling tool, with Smalltalk, C++, and database Data Definition Language (DDL), generated as an output of the tool.

In this fashion, the client and server components of the application are created simultaneously. As the work develops, the client and server development teams agree on well-defined interfaces that will support the needs of the clients with the services and data available on the server. These interfaces may also be published in such a fashion as to be made available for use by other existing or future applications.

The goal of the client developers is usability and making the information available to the users to meet their transactional requirements. That is, the screens should be designed to meet the needs of the optimal number of users but also have the flexibility to meet the needs of all the possible users. The goal of the server developers is to create business objects that will last and be leverageable into future applications.

Given the power of client GUI development tools, the server developer also needs modeling tools. The best result is also obtained if both the client and server interface definitions and stubs are built using the output from a server modeling tool. Further leverage can be gained by the interface browser interacting directly with the repository that contains the interface definitions, which are directly generated by the modeling tool.

The problem of client/server DOT development is fairly simple when compared to multiple servers supporting multiple clients, in a so-called multitier fashion. When a client accesses a server, which itself is a client to another server and so on, understanding the problem from a business perspective can become complex. Happily, object encapsulation and its subsequent simplification of inherent complexity are of help here.

Any problem, algorithm, or procedure is more complex than may be initially presented. It is initially important to a particular user to understand a given object and its interfaces to the degree necessary to determine if the object contains information or functionality that is of value to him. In a distributed system, it is valuable for a business or technology analyst to understand what objects (methods and data) reside in given locations on the network. In the same way that the World Wide Web is an assortment of reference information and services, so too is the network of servers in a business an assortment of transactional systems and reference sources.

What is needed to effectively model and create applications in a distributed environment are visualization tools that depict what services are available in what locations. These browsers may be hyperlinked in Web fashion to one another so that a service documented on one machine that uses a service on another machine provides a link to learn about that other machine's service. As new services emerge, they are added to the browsers and made available for viewing.

In this sense, strong links need to be made and maintained between the activity of creating applications as well as the implementation of applications. It is well known what happens to laboriously developed computer models of information systems if the models are not linked both forward and backward with the actual implementations. The models gather dust on a bookshelf or a disk-based repository, never to be viewed again.

Inasmuch as models are linked to their implementations, either via code generation or active implementation repositories, the models are kept up to date.

CAN DOT ENABLE I-CASE FOR CLIENT/SERVER?

An integrated system is more valuable than one that has to be pieced together. For some time now, and not just in the CASE arena, there has been the argument between integrated systems and environments and *best of breed* environments. The power of integrated environments is, of course, in their ease of use and ability to make movement from one phase of system development to another more seamless. The weakness of integrated environments is that they can't do the best of everything. An I-CASE tool may have a great modeling and code generation package but be sorely lacking in the GUI building and client/server middleware area. In order to fully utilize the I-CASE tool, then, compromises are necessary or else the tool has to be *broken apart* to use the high-value components with other tools that were not made to work with the environment.

The other solution is to use *best of breed* tools. Pick the best modeling tool, the best code generation tool, the best GUI builder, the best middleware solution, etc. Then, paste them all together and *poof* — your own customized I-CASE environment. The only problem is that the pasting is not all that easy and, since technology is changing continuously, you are going to have to paste again in a year or 18 months.

Distributed object technology is of help in both cases here. As I-CASE vendors encapsulate their tools with object interfaces, the ability of customers to fit in other components is made easier. As I-CASE vendors embrace CORBA or Distributed OLE technologies, the use of I-CASE tools to support distributed environments is enhanced. Benefits are enhanced in a similar fashion for providers of component tools that may be used in a *best of breed* strategy. As these providers enhance their tools to export object interfaces, especially distributed object interfaces, they simplify the tasks of customers in piecing together environments that work well together.

For example, assume a user is using an I-CASE environment, such as Information Engineering Facility (IEF) from Texas Instruments. The IEF was originally designed to support client/server environments but only with its own GUI builder. It was possible to create your own GUIs using, for example, Powerbuilder or Visual-Works Smalltalk, but then you had to build your own *network glue.* It was possible to do that, and in fact, some people inside HP did just that. They used the IEF to generate server code and threw away the client code that was generated. They used an advanced GUI tool on the client and used in-house code and methods to generate the middleware code and interfaces between the client and the server. In the case of Smalltalk, the in-house tool, known as OSCAR (On-line Service Catalog and Repository), generated Smalltalk class libraries so that client developers could easily access server facilities with little effort.

Many CASE vendors are now finding ways to make their tools more open and more easily integrated with other tools. In order to make these CASE environments full partners in the distributed object arena, there will need to be provision made for lifecycle, naming, request broker, and other key DOT services. CASE tools that support these services will find customers and other ISVs moving quickly to integrate their tools with other DOT applications and tools.

KEY ISSUES IN TEAM DEVELOPMENT

As discussed earlier in the chapter, the DOT/CASE combination has some implications for team development. First among these is specialization. The kind of specialization brought about by client/server is amplified in a DOT environment. Client/server teams may tend to revolve around client developers and server developers. Client developers will tend to focus on rapid prototyping GUI development, user interface standards, and optimization, etc. Server developers will focus more on effective representation of business objects, effective database access, exporting reusable interfaces, etc.

DOT takes the matter further. In a DOT environment, there may well be a person focusing on effective reuse of distributed objects. More and more applications will use combinations of components that already exist. The client developer will focus on combining components from a library of components. In the same way that today's client developers use libraries of GUI components (scroll bars, edit boxes, etc.), DOT client developers will use libraries of GUI business components, such as name/address boxes, product information controls, order entry controls, etc. These controls will be available in much the same way as existing GUI controls. The difference is, these business components will be designed to be easily connected to their respective server component counterparts. That is, when a client developer *drags* an order entry control to a window while building an application, the knowledge of how to get to the proper server object is dragged along with it.

The server developer's job is altered by DOT too. As CASE tools evolve to support DOT, server developers will need to worry less about the middleware needed to access their business objects. The CASE tool can generate DOT standard compliant interfaces and be assured that client components can get to them. The CASE tools can also generate the client side GUI components that can be used by the client developer. The actual implementation language of the client is of less importance because the client object can be implemented in a language other than that of the client GUI tool. On the client, an ORB can connect the GUI component object with the controlling application. The application can be generated in Smalltalk, then, for example, while the GUI component itself may actually be written in C++. The Smalltalk application, even on the client, then, may be accessing the component using a local, fast-path ORB.

14

MANAGEMENT OF DISTRIBUTED OBJECT SYSTEMS

Management of distributed systems is a complicated task. On any given network there may be dozens of servers with hundreds or thousands of clients and users. Each user may run numerous, different applications that access the servers in different ways. There are outside servers accessed internally. There are numerous routers, bridges, and hubs on the network that need to be configured and controlled. The applications on the clients and servers need to be configured, their versions monitored and managed. System and network interrupts need to be monitored and logged. Management information must be derived from the output of the network and system monitoring tools to facilitate expansion or changes in the network infrastructure.

Into this mix come applications that now allow users to access more fine-grained objects than ever before. They allow users more flexibility in how they access information. They give users more ability to access reporting information on-line.

This situation is not uncommon today. As more companies move from traditional mainframe environments to client/server environments, the management difficulties compound. Distributed object technology will make the manager's job even more difficult by enabling software developers to make more effective use of client/server technology, causing more network traffic, interactions between clients and servers, and giving users more capabilities (and therefore need) to access their systems.

Distributed object technology is also a benefit for the system manager. Most modern network and systems management tools use some measure of distributed object technology as a foundation. Indeed, the network and systems management problem may in some respects be the premier application of distributed object technology.

To a DOT-based network and systems management tool, each item on a network is an object. Servers, clients, applications, databases, network devices, network cabling, and even users, can be represented effectively in an object system. With distributed object technology, a systems management tool can inquire on the status of a remote machine or piece of equipment. With event services, machines, applications, or users on the network can send alerts to the system management tool, or the tool can poll the network for status. Naming services provide a more consistent means for system software developers, application developers, and administrators to structure, store, and access object information.

GUIs are of great benefit in helping technical users visualize the complexity and intricacy of a network. The relationships between major nodes can be depicted, then broken down into finer-grained detail. Relationships can be depicted. Related hardware and software can be selected off pop-up menus. These GUIs can be generated by automatic discovery mechanisms that search the network and establish the relationships shown on the screen. DOT is of significant help in producing all of these results. Each major node is an object consisting of many subobjects. Each subobject is also a collection of smaller objects, etc. The discovery mechanism can be an object service that sends discovery events to objects on the network that respond back with callback events to announce their presence and status.

SYSTEM MANAGEMENT STANDARDS

One of the most significant requirements for a distributed systems and network management facility to function correctly is for standard interfaces to exist on the network for the resources being managed. It is encouraging that such standards have been developed, and that more object-oriented standards are being developed. The X/Open Systems Management Working Group (SysMan) "has been working for over two years on the specification of a CORBA environment based object oriented framework for building managed objects and systems management applications" ("Resolution of Issues Related to the XCMF RFC," OMG document 95-12-09).

SysMan's *System Management: Common Management Facilities*, Volume 1, Version 2 (XCMF2) (OMG documents 95-12-03 through 95-12-06) documents a Management Facilities Architecture and Specification, including a Managed Set Service, Policy-driven Base Service, Instance Management Services, and Policy Management Service. Each of these services has interfaces documented using CORBA IDL.

While system management standards have historically been a quagmire, it may yet be hoped that as this RFC becomes accepted and pervasive, there will be an increasing ability for component object development for management of applications, network devices, system management applications, etc. This overall trend would improve data center managers' ability to find products and solutions to meet their needs. There is still much more room for improvement, of course, but steps such as XCMF move very much in the right direction.

15

THE ORGANIZATION AND DOT

At Hewlett-Packard, as well as at most well-managed companies, the contribution of individual employees is not to be overstated or underappreciated. The more highly a company regards its employees — both in terms of authority and *privilege,* as well as in terms of responsibility — the more it will get out of those employees. Empowering the individual contributor to make the most out of his or her position is a key differentiator in a very competitive business landscape.

It is obvious that when a corporate executive or staff person has significant access to high value information sources, the company benefits — the executive or staff person makes and influences decisions that may impact the whole company. It is less obvious but nevertheless true that people *on the line* or in the field bring no less benefit to the company when they also have easy and effective access to high-value information. When an *order entry clerk* becomes an *order manager* and has access to information that will both make the customer happy (expedite the order, etc.) and relieve the burden of the sales representative, the cumulative orders that are saved may bring as much additional business to the company as some executive decision from headquarters.

The point here is that ready access to any sort of information — information that may only be interesting to one *line* person in the company and therefore not worth the effort of the IS department — is facilitated by DOT. This ready access to information makes the line person — any line person — more effective and productive. This means fewer line people can do more work and fewer managers are needed, fewer staff people, etc. Hewlett-Packard, for example, has gone from around $10 billion a year to over $30 billion a year in just a few years with practically no increase in employee headcount, in large part because people are working smarter and doing higher-value work. A significant contributor to this has been the effective use of information technology. Distributed object technology will be an even more useful tool in this environment, overcoming some of the limitations of the file servers, database and application servers, and imaging servers now in use.

EVOLVING THE IS CULTURE

As with integration of any new technology, cultural changes need to occur to enable the most effective implementation and use of that technology. Today, many developers and managers in IS shops spend their time integrating technologies from various sources both inside and outside the company. This integration of accounting with manufacturing and personnel with management planning and retail/field sales with research and development and marketing at both the business and technology levels takes considerable time and money. DOT will not eliminate the need for this activity but will attenuate it somewhat. More developers and managers will be able to spend more of their time on straight business issues rather than on integration issues because of two factors.

First, more software will be purchased in the future than in previous years and this software will be easier to integrate into the IS environment because of standards like DOT and be more usable more quickly because of DOT. Second, software developed in-house will be easier to integrate with other in-house software because DOT and other standards have uncovered the appropriate abstractions and interfaces for clients, servers, networks, databases, and applications (naming, events, transactions, etc.). When accounting uses a naming service, manufacturing can more readily use that interface than if accounting writes a home-grown directory system that adheres to no standards and then requires manufacturing to mold its needs to that directory system.

ENNOBLING END USERS

End users, the customers of IS and software vendors, have traditionally been treated as somewhat less sophisticated in their use of technology than the developers were. This was completely understandable ten, or even five, years ago. When users had only very limited TSO or CICS menu or line-mode interfaces to relatively basic applications, while programmers had the PL/1 checkout compiler, IMS, VSAM, and SPF, it was safe to say that developers had a better grasp on technology than end users did.

Things are different now. Millions of people have graphical user interfaces at home. While many developers have a somewhat detailed knowledge of the internals of these interfaces and can talk in detail about window messages and callbacks and database interfaces, there is really too much information available today for even a dedicated software developer to stay on top of all of it. Much of what even developers know is related more to using a tool than the internals of it.

While I once understood very well the internal data structures and overall functional structure of some operating systems, today I must limit myself more and more to understanding only more abstract levels of the operating system. While I once had detailed knowledge of terminal handling protocols, I must now limit myself to understanding the APIs that interface to the GUI on my desktop (or in the case of Smalltalk, to classes that abstract the APIs). That is, today I must limit myself to not understanding the internals as much as understanding the interfaces to the OS or the subsystem or DBMS or GUI environment.

This commitment to the interface is at the heart of DOT. Indeed, it was the first standard agreed upon with IDL in CORBA 1.0 and is at the heart of the success of OLE and the use of HTML in the Web community. Now, rather than being highly concerned with fine-tuning applications to fully utilize all of the available MIPs and bandwidth of a piece of hardware, we are now more interested in its portability and interoperability. While performance will always be an important issue, it is more incumbent on the systems and OS vendors to make their portable interfaces perform better, and relative to years ago, less an issue for the customer to worry so much about.

As business systems are more and more accessible via user-accessible object-oriented interfaces, published and available over a network, users will be able to accomplish a greater amount of work without significant technical assistance. This will elevate users to "nobility" status and remove creation of even moderately complex applications from the realm of the *wizards*.

16

WHERE IS DOT GOING?

The information systems world is slowly evolving to a distributed object technology paradigm. Microsoft has begun to move the desktop world in that direction with OLE. The major systems vendors like HP, IBM, Sun, etc., have begun to move the server world in that direction with CORBA. The Internet community has begun to move that way with Web browsers, HTTP, CGI, etc.. It is, quite simply, the case that the world is moving to objects and networks, which means network-based or distributed objects.

What are the implications for such a move? This book has described just a portion of the broad array of distributed object technologies that are available and in production sites right now. While it is true that DOT applications are not pervasive, it is also true that they will be. It can be no other way. Until a better way of developing distributed applications comes along, DOT is the best game in town. The next sections explore what the transition to DOT will look like in the months and years to come.

AN ERA OF OBJECT ASSEMBLY PLUG AND PLAY

Today, you can buy a spreadsheet from vendor A that will plug into a word processor from vendor B, even though they weren't designed with each other in mind. That is fairly straightforward since word processors are well known and so are spreadsheets. Tomorrow, you will be able to buy an accounting package that will plug into a purchasing package, even though they weren't specifically designed to work together. Further, for example, since your accounting department uses an HP-UX box, that is where you put the accounting package. Since the purchasing department uses an NT server, you install the purchasing package on Windows NT and the two packages work together over the network just fine. This is the promise of DOT.

Imagine, as well, buying an add-on to the purchasing package that only runs on Oracle (with object extensions, of course), which you have only licensed for your HP-UX box. Rather than buy Oracle for NT, Accounting agrees to put the package on their UNIX box for Purchasing. It, too, can access the rest of the purchasing package (on NT) via DOT. Your users don't even know, in addition, that the new purchasing piece isn't on the NT server. All they know is that it's available and they can get to it. And you didn't even need to handcraft anything. This environment is depicted in Figure 16–1.

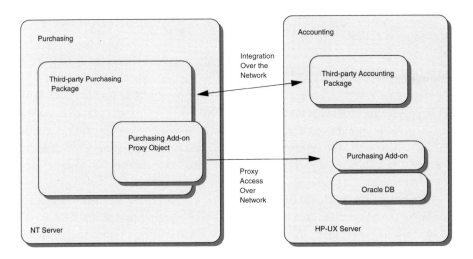

Figure 16–1. Distributed object interaction involving two hardware platforms and two software packages

OPPORTUNITIES FOR SELLING EXPERTISE
THROUGH COMPONENTS OBJECTS

There are specific strengths of expertise going underutilized today. A scientist with expertise in business metrics contracts with a consulting firm to develop an application that captures her knowledge, but the consulting firm is limited to certain platforms or types of development tools in its implementation of the scientists' expertise. An expert programmer uncovers some new ways of generating financial instruments but is limited to a few implementations of his ideas because of the many different operating systems and languages and network interfaces and so on.

In *Patterns of Problem Solving* (Moshe F. Rubinstein, Prentice Hall, 1975), Dr. Moshe Rubinstein said that there are two main difficulties in problem solving: failure to use known information and introduction of unnecessary constraints. In the information systems business, we have been hamstrung by these two difficulties almost since the beginning. The moment there were two different operating systems or two different languages or two different network interfaces, unnecessary constraints were introduced. These constraints led in addition to failure to use known information. If today I have a great word processor that I want to link to an outstanding knowledge-based system that I would like to connect to some very useful databases, the likelihood is high that some constraint exists preventing me from doing just that. My subsequent inability to integrate objects from these resources results in failure to use known information.

CORBA, OLE, and the Web are steps in the right direction of creating the right abstractions and the right interfaces to remove a considerable number of the constraints that have been plaguing the information technology business from the start. While it is certain that we have not uncovered *all* of the right abstractions, we have uncovered a great many of them. We now have the right mix to allow highly specialized and brilliant men and women to begin to share their expertise with the rest of us without having to worry about the specific implementation. If one of them wants to implement the application on UNIX using Informix with Smalltalk, that's just fine. The rest of the applications in the world can access it. The evolution of DOT will include elements of OLE, CORBA, and Web services, all melded into a cohesive, interoperable, widely used set of integrated standards. The result will draw on strengths from all of them — document interfaces from OLE, object services from CORBA, and network interfaces from all three.

REVOLUTION IN NEWS REPORTING

The widespread and growing use of the Web has already shown a glimpse of the future in information distribution. Many news sources are available today to anyone who cares to look for them. As the mechanisms for payment of services become more standard and trusted, the deployment and use of such on-line information sources will become more prevalent and pervasive. Consumer pilot projects such as 25-megabit bandwidth over cable television lines are being carried out even now. If George Gilder and others are correct, the nearly limitless bandwidth of fiber optic cable will further feed the news revolution.

While it will be hardware in the form of faster processors and wider band-width and lower costs all around that will provide the foundation of the new era of news reporting, it is object technology that will truly facilitate the power and wide-spread use of the new hardware. If the same old *mainframelike* distribution mecha-nism is present in the new era, much potential will be wasted. People want more than just limited information from a few sources, such as the major networks. Instead, the new era will be marked by situations where one person in one possibly remote place in the country or the world will put a bit of information on-line — whether it be simple text, a sound bite, or a video clip — and that information will be accessed by one other person in very different circumstances.

This return to a truly global village (not to belabor an old phrase), where indi-viduals provide information to individuals — uncensored, unfiltered, channeled from one place to another solely by virtue of its content — will herald an unprecedented time of freedom of thought and (hopefully) virtue of action.

HOLLYWOOD OBJECTS

Entertainment will benefit from DOT. While the primary beneficiaries of DOT will initially be business, followed by public news and information distribution services, entertainment will follow. Entertainment is the most difficult, partly because it nec-essarily means video and sound, and secondly because the level of entry is so high. People expect a great deal from entertainment. Movies and television (even video games) suffer today from a limitation on the means of distribution. In some ways, entertainment executives are like the robber barons of the days when the railroad was supreme. It wasn't that the railroads were bad; they were just limited and their use was controlled to benefit a few. Today, entertainment is in the *railroad* stage. Other people decide what *trains* (movies/shows) run at what time in what place — your only choice is when to get on board (if you want to get on board).

The entertainment business of the future is like the highway system. If you want to go from your house to anywhere else in the country, you just get in your car and go. The way you navigate the highway is completely up to you — it is merely a public accessway.

Here again, the benefit is this: Say you have a particular entertainment inter-est that is not widespread such as kite flying contests. Today, you are out of luck. You may have a magazine or two for your interest, but a *kite flying channel*? Not likely. Down the road, however, once we all have access to each other's personal clients and servers, someone may just put up a kite flying video server. This server wouldn't need to actually store all the videos. Via object links, the server may just hold connections to all sorts of other servers that have the actual video data. It may just be a *kite flying video* broker server.

This sort of thing could be carried into almost any interest area. If you are a home builder, when you come home, you don't see Peter Jennings any more. You see Ralph Henderson, a large, successful general contractor, who has showmanship in him and goes to the trouble of putting on a ten-minute news video each day bringing up-to-date news on the construction business. Ralph is followed by various other text and video clips that your home information server found out on the networks while you were at work.

What does this have to do with distributed object technology, you might ask? The answer is this: The kinds of technologies being standardized, developed, and deployed — ORBs, events, naming services, transaction services, etc. — will be a standard requirement before the kinds of entertainment changes discussed here can become truly usable and pervasive. In the area of network and systems management alone, current, nonobject-based technologies are being stretched beyond their limits as software developers, systems manufacturers, and systems administrators try to keep up with the explosive growth of networks just in their own companies. Network and systems management vendors and users are some of the very first to really grasp and deploy the significant leverage brought by use of distributed object technology.

After network and system management, software developers will need DOT to be able to develop the kinds of applications that can be widely deployed and easily used by the mass market. If infinite bandwidth were available today for home use, Ralph Henderson would still not find his widest audience because of the many different standards for video, file sharing, and network interfaces. Ralph may develop and deploy his video news clips (or live feeds) using a UNIX server. Many of his audience may be using Windows 95 or Macintosh clients. With DOT standard interfaces, all the bases are covered with respect to finding information, *contracting* for the information (via IDL type interfaces), supporting transactions for payment, and the like.

CONCLUSION

The future is bright for the continued use and improvement of information technology. Distributed object technology has a key role to play in that future. With DOT, vendors, software developers, end users, and consumers will all gain networked applications that are easier to facilitate, develop, and use. Objects are here to stay. Networks are the way of the future. Networks with objects have great synergy when put together. DOT will become as common and pervasive as coffee makers, and as unobtrusive. The technologies in this book are only the kernel. The full fruit will be born out of time and care.

BIBLIOGRAPHY

CHORAFAS, DIMITRIS N., and STEINMANN, HEINRICH. *Object-Oriented Databases.* Englewood Cliffs, NJ: PTR Prentice Hall, 1993.

COLEMAN, D., ARNOLD, P., BODOFF, S., DOLLIN C., GILCHRIST, H., HAYES, F., and JEREMAES, P., *Object-Oriented Development: The Fusion Method.* Englewood Cliffs, NJ: Prentice Hall, 1994.

GAMMA, E., HELM, R., JOHNSON, R., and VLISSIDES, J. *Design Patterns.* Reading, MA: Addison-Wesley, 1994.

GILDER, GEORGE. *Life After Television.* New York, NY: WW. Norton and Company, 1992.

HEWLETT-PACKARD COMPANY. *Odapter/OpenODB Reference Document.* HP Part number B3768-90020. Palo Alto, CA: Hewlett-Packard, 1995.

IONA TECHNOLOGIES INC. *Orbix Microsoft Windows with OLE Integration Programmer's Guide.* Marlboro, MA: Iona Technologies Inc., 1995.

KHANNA, RAMAN. *Distributed Computing.* Englewood Cliffs, NJ: PTR Prentice Hall, 1994.

LALONDE, WILF R., and PUGH, JOHN R. *Inside Smalltalk, Volume 1.* Englewood Cliffs, NJ: Prentice Hall, 1990.

MICROSOFT CORPORATION. *OLE2 Programmer's Reference, Volume One Working with Windows Objects.* Redmond, WA: Microsoft Corporation, 1994.

MICROSOFT CORPORATION. *OLE2 Programmer's Reference, Volume Two Creating Programmable Applications with OLE Automation.* Redmond, WA: Microsoft Corporation, 1994.

MICROSOFT CORPORATION. *Building Client/Server Applications with Visual Basic.* Redmond, WA: Microsoft Corporation, 1995.

MICROSOFT CORPORATION. *Microsoft Visual Basic Language Reference.* Redmond, WA: Microsoft Corporation, 1995.

MOWBRAY, THOMAS J. and ZAHAVI, RON. *The Essential CORBA, Systems Integration Using Distributed Objects.* New York, NY: John Wiley and Sons, 1995.

OBJECT MANAGEMENT GROUP. *The Common Object Request Broker: Architecture and Specification.* John Wiley and Sons, Inc. 1992a.

OBJECT MANAGEMENT GROUP. *Common Object Services Specifications.* John Wiley and Sons, Inc. 1994.

RUBINSTEIN, MOSHE F. *Patterns of Problem Solving.* Englewood Cliffs, NJ: Prentice Hall, 1975.

TAYLOR, DAVID A. *Object-Oriented Information Systems.* New York, NY: John Wiley and Sons, 1992.

TAYLOR, DAVID A. *Object-Oriented Technology: A Manager's Guide.* Reading, MA: Addison-Wesley, 1990.

INDEX